ASIAN POLITICAL, ECONOMIC AND SECURITY ISSUES

MALAYSIA: COUNTRY PROFILE AND U.S. RELATIONS

ASIAN POLITICAL, ECONOMIC AND SECURITY ISSUES

Additional books in this series can be found on Nova's website under the Series tab.

Additional E-books in this series can be found on Nova's website under the E-books tab.

Asian Political, Economic and Security Issues

Malaysia: Country Profile and U.S. Relations

Gabriela A. Villalobos
and
Daniel E. Segura
Editors

Nova Science Publishers, Inc.
New York

Copyright © 2011 by Nova Science Publishers, Inc.

All rights reserved. No part of this book may be reproduced, stored in a retrieval system or transmitted in any form or by any means: electronic, electrostatic, magnetic, tape, mechanical photocopying, recording or otherwise without the written permission of the Publisher.

For permission to use material from this book please contact us:
Telephone 631-231-7269; Fax 631-231-8175
Web Site: http://www.novapublishers.com

NOTICE TO THE READER

The Publisher has taken reasonable care in the preparation of this book, but makes no expressed or implied warranty of any kind and assumes no responsibility for any errors or omissions. No liability is assumed for incidental or consequential damages in connection with or arising out of information contained in this book. The Publisher shall not be liable for any special, consequential, or exemplary damages resulting, in whole or in part, from the readers' use of, or reliance upon, this material. Any parts of this book based on government reports are so indicated and copyright is claimed for those parts to the extent applicable to compilations of such works.

Independent verification should be sought for any data, advice or recommendations contained in this book. In addition, no responsibility is assumed by the publisher for any injury and/or damage to persons or property arising from any methods, products, instructions, ideas or otherwise contained in this publication.

This publication is designed to provide accurate and authoritative information with regard to the subject matter covered herein. It is sold with the clear understanding that the Publisher is not engaged in rendering legal or any other professional services. If legal or any other expert assistance is required, the services of a competent person should be sought. FROM A DECLARATION OF PARTICIPANTS JOINTLY ADOPTED BY A COMMITTEE OF THE AMERICAN BAR ASSOCIATION AND A COMMITTEE OF PUBLISHERS.

Additional color graphics may be available in the e-book version of this book.

Library of Congress Cataloging-in-Publication Data

Malaysia : country profile and U.S. relations / editors, Gabriela A. Villalobos and Daniel E. Segura.
   p. cm. -- (Asian political, economic and security issues)
   Includes bibliographical references and index.
   ISBN 978-1-61470-172-9 (softcover)
 1. United States--Foreign relations--Malaysia. 2. Malaysia--Foreign relations--United States. 3. Malaysia--Politics and government--21st century. I. Villalobos, Gabriela A. II. Segura, Daniel E. III. Series: Asian political, economic and security issues.
   E183.8.M4M34 2011
   327.730595--dc23
                         2011020774

Published by Nova Science Publishers, Inc. † *New York*

CONTENTS

Preface		vii
Chapter 1	Malaysian Profile *United States Department of State*	1
Chapter 2	U.S.-Malaysia Relations: Implications of the 2008 Elections *Michael F. Martin*	11
Chapter 3	The Proposed U.S.-Malaysia Free Trade Agreement *Michael F. Martin*	51
Chapter 4	Malaysia: Country Analysis Briefs *Energy Information Administration*	95
Index		107

PREFACE

The United States and Malaysia have enjoyed a positive trade relationship over the last few years, in part because both nations favor trade and investment liberalization in Asia. Malaysia is the United States' 10th largest trading partner. Building on their common perspective of international trade, Malaysia and the United States concluded a trade and investment framework agreement in 2004 and are currently negotiating a bilateral free trade agreement. This book discusses key aspects of the U.S.-Malaysia relationship (including economics and trade, counterterrorism cooperation and defense ties), and the possible impact of Malaysia's 2008 elections on the future of the relationship.

Chapter 1- Malaysia's predominant political party, the United Malays National Organization (UMNO), has held power in coalition with other parties continuously since independence in 1957. The UMNO coalition's share of the vote declined in national elections held in May 1969, after which riots broke out in Kuala Lumpur and elsewhere, mainly between Malays and ethnic Chinese. Several hundred people were killed or injured. The government declared a state of emergency and suspended all parliamentary activities.

Chapter 2- This report discusses key aspects of the U.S.-Malaysia relationship (including economics and trade, counterterrorism cooperation, and defense ties) and the possible impact of Malaysia's 2008 elections on the future of the relationship.

In parliamentary elections held on March 8, 2008, the Barisan Nasional (BN), which has ruled Malaysia since independence in 1957, was struck by a "political tsunami" that saw it lose its two-thirds "supermajority" for the first time since 1969. Malaysia's major opposition parties won 82 of the 222 parliamentary seats up for election. In addition, the opposition parties won control of five of Malaysia's 13 state governments. The election results are widely seen as a vote against the current policies of the Malaysian government, which could have implications for relations with the United States.

Chapter 3- This report addresses the proposed U.S.-Malaysia free trade agreement (FTA). It provides an overview of the current status of the negotiations, a review of the 2008 talks, an examination of leading issues that have arisen during the negotiations, a review of U.S. interests in the proposed agreement, a summary of the potential effects of a FTA on bilateral trade, and an overview of the legislative procedures to be followed if the proposed FTA is presented to Congress for approval.

Chapter 4- Although Malaysia's oil fields are maturing, new offshore developments of both oil and gas are expected to increase aggregate production capacity in the near- to mid-term. Malaysia's western coast runs alongside the Strait of Malacca, an important route for seaborne energy trade that links the Indian and Pacific Oceans.

In: Malaysia: Country Profile and U.S. Relations   ISBN: 978-1-61470-172-9
Editors: G. A. Villalobos, D. E. Segura © 2011 Nova Science Publishers, Inc.

Chapter 1

MALAYSIAN PROFILE[*]

United States Department of State

Flag of Malaysia

GEOGRAPHY

Area: 329,847 sq. km. (127,315 sq. mi.); slightly larger than New Mexico.

Cities: *Capital*--Kuala Lumpur. *Other cities*--Penang, Ipoh, Malacca, Johor Baru, Shah Alam, Klang, Kuching, Kota Kinabalu, Kota Baru, Kuala Terengganu, Miri, Petaling Jaya.

Terrain: Coastal plains and interior, jungle-covered mountains. The South China Sea separates peninsular Malaysia from East Malaysia on Borneo.

Climate: Tropical.

---

[*] This is an edited, reformatted and augmented version of the United States Department of State publication, from http://www.state, dated October 2010.

PEOPLE

Nationality: *Noun and adjective*--Malaysian(s).
Population (2010): 28.3 million.
Annual population growth rate: 1.7%.
Ethnic groups: Malay 53.3%, Chinese 26.0%, indigenous 11.8%, Indian 7.7%, others 1.2%.
Religions: Islam (60.4%), Buddhism (19.2%), Christianity (9.1%), Hinduism (6.3%), other/none (5.0%).
Languages: Bahasa Melayu (official), Chinese (various dialects), English, Tamil, indigenous.
Education: *Years compulsory*--6. *Attendance*--90.1% (primary), 60.0% (secondary). *Literacy*--93.5%.
Health: *Infant mortality rate* (2007)--6.7/1,000. *Life expectancy* (2007)--female 76.4 yrs., male 71.9 yrs.
Work force (10.89 million, 2007): *Services*--57%; *industry*--28% (*manufacturing*--19%, *mining and construction*--9%); *agriculture*--15%.

GOVERNMENT

Type: Federal parliamentary democracy with a constitutional monarch.
Independence: August 31, 1957. (Malaya, which is now peninsular Malaysia, became independent in 1957. In 1963 Malaya, Sabah, Sarawak, and Singapore formed Malaysia. Singapore became an independent country in 1965.)
Constitution: 1957.
Subdivisions: 13 states and three federal territories (Kuala Lumpur, Labuan Island, Putrajaya federal administrative territory). Each state has an assembly and government headed by a chief minister. Nine of these states have hereditary rulers, generally titled "sultans," while the remaining four have appointed governors in counterpart positions.
Branches: *Executive*--Yang di-Pertuan Agong (head of state and customarily referred to as the king; has ceremonial duties), prime minister (head of government), cabinet. *Legislative*--bicameral parliament, comprising 70-member Senate (26 elected by the 13 state assemblies, 44 appointed by the king on the prime minister's recommendation) and 222-member House of Representatives (elected from single-member districts). *Judicial*--Federal

Court, Court of Appeals, high courts, session's courts, magistrate's courts, and juvenile courts. Sharia courts hear cases on certain matters involving Muslims only.

Political parties: Barisan Nasional (National Front)--a coalition comprising the United Malays National Organization (UMNO) and 12 other parties, most of which are ethnically based; Democratic Action Party (DAP); Parti Islam se Malaysia (PAS); Parti Keadilan Rakyat Malaysia (PKR). There are more than 30 registered political parties, including the foregoing, not all of which are represented in the federal parliament.

Suffrage: Universal adult (voting age 21).

Economy (2009)

Nominal GDP: $191.5 billion.

Annual real GDP growth rate: 5.9% (2006); 6.3% (2007); 4.6% (2008); -1.7% (2009); 7.0% (government estimate for 2010).

Nominal per capita income (GNI): $6,897.

Natural resources: Petroleum, liquefied natural gas (LNG), tin, minerals.

Agricultural products: Palm oil, rubber, timber, cocoa, rice, tropical fruit, fish, coconut.

Industry: *Types*--electronics, electrical products, chemicals, food and beverages, metal and machine products, apparel.

Trade: *Merchandise exports*--$180.8 billion: electronic products, machinery, liquid natural gas, petroleum and petroleum products, telecom equipment. *Major markets*--Singapore 14.0%, China 12.2%, U.S. 11.0%, Japan 9.8%. *Merchandise imports*--$142.1 billion: electronic products, machinery, machinery parts and apparatus, petroleum and petroleum products. *Major suppliers*--China 14.0%, Japan 12.5%, U.S. 11.2%, Singapore 11.1%.

PEOPLE

Malaysia's multi-racial society contains many ethnic groups. Malays comprise a majority of just over 50%. By constitutional definition, all Malays are Muslim. About a quarter of the population is ethnic Chinese, a group which historically played an important role in trade and business. Malaysians of Indian descent comprise about 7% of the population and include Hindus, Muslims, Buddhists, and Christians. Non-Malay indigenous groups combine to make up approximately 11% of the population.

Population density is highest in peninsular Malaysia, home to some 20 million of the country's 28 million inhabitants. The rest live on the Malaysian portion of the island of Borneo in the large but less densely-populated states of Sabah and Sarawak. More than half of Sarawak's residents and about two-thirds of Sabah's are from indigenous groups.

HISTORY

The early Buddhist Malay kingdom of Srivijaya, based at what is now Palembang, Sumatra, dominated much of the Malay peninsula from the 9th to the 13th centuries AD. The powerful Hindu kingdom of Majapahit, based on Java, gained control of the Malay peninsula in the 14th century. Conversion of the Malays to Islam, beginning in the early 14th century, accelerated with the rise of the state of Malacca under the rule of a Muslim prince in the 15th century. Malacca was a major regional commercial center, where Chinese, Arab, Malay, and Indian merchants traded precious goods.

Drawn by this rich trade, a Portuguese fleet conquered Malacca in 1511, marking the beginning of European expansion in Southeast Asia. The Dutch ousted the Portuguese from Malacca in 1641. The British obtained the island of Penang in 1786 and temporarily controlled Malacca with Dutch acquiescence from 1795 to 1818 to prevent it from falling to the French during the Napoleonic war. The British gained lasting possession of Malacca from the Dutch in 1824, through the Anglo-Dutch treaty, in exchange for territory on the island of Sumatra in what is today Indonesia.

In 1826, the British settlements of Malacca, Penang, and Singapore were combined to form the Colony of the Straits Settlements. From these strongholds, in the 19th and early 20th centuries the British established protectorates over the Malay sultanates on the peninsula. During their rule the British developed large-scale rubber and tin production and established a system of public administration. British control was interrupted by World War II and the Japanese occupation from 1941 to 1945.

Popular sentiment for independence swelled during and after the war. The territories of peninsular Malaysia joined together to form the Federation of Malaya in 1948 and eventually negotiated independence from the British in 1957. Tunku Abdul Rahman became the first prime minister. In 1963 the British colonies of Singapore, Sarawak, and Sabah joined the Federation, which was renamed Malaysia. Singapore's membership was short-lived, however; it left in 1965 and became an independent republic.

Neighboring Indonesia objected to the formation of Malaysia and began a program of economic, political, diplomatic, and military "confrontation" against the new country in 1963, which ended only after the fall of Indonesia's President Sukarno in 1966. Internally, local communists, nearly all Chinese, carried out a long, bitter insurgency both before and after independence, prompting the imposition of a state of emergency from 1948 to 1960. Small bands of guerrillas remained in bases along the rugged border with southern Thailand, occasionally entering northern Malaysia. These guerrillas finally signed a peace accord with the Malaysian Government in December 1989. A separate, small-scale communist insurgency that began in the mid-1960s in Sarawak also ended with the signing of a peace accord in October 1990.

GOVERNMENT

Malaysia is a constitutional monarchy, nominally headed by the Yang di-Pertuan Agong, customarily referred to as the king. The king is elected for 5-year terms from among the nine sultans of the peninsular Malaysian states. The king also is the leader of the Islamic faith in Malaysia.

Executive power is vested in the cabinet led by the prime minister; the Malaysian constitution stipulates that the prime minister must be a member of the lower house of parliament who, in the opinion of the Yang di-Pertuan Agong, commands a majority in parliament. The cabinet is chosen from among members of both houses of parliament and is responsible to that body.

The bicameral parliament consists of the Senate (Dewan Negara) and the House of Representatives (Dewan Rakyat). All 70 Senate members sit for 3-year terms, which are normally extended for an additional 3 years; 26 are elected by the 13 state assemblies, and 44 are appointed by the king following the prime minister's recommendation. Representatives of the House are elected from single-member districts by universal adult suffrage. The 222 members of the House of Representatives are elected to parliamentary terms lasting up to 5 years. Legislative power is divided between federal and state legislatures.

The Malaysian legal system is based on English common law. The Federal Court reviews decisions referred from the Court of Appeal; it has original jurisdiction in constitutional matters and in disputes between states or between the federal government and a state. Peninsular Malaysia and the East Malaysian states of Sabah and Sarawak each have a high court.

The federal government has authority over external affairs, defense, internal security, justice (except civil law cases among Malays or other Muslims and other indigenous peoples, adjudicated under Islamic and traditional law), federal citizenship, finance, commerce, industry, communications, transportation, and other matters.

PRINCIPAL GOVERNMENT OFFICIALS

Prime Minister--Mohd Najib bin Abdul Razak
Foreign Minister--Anifah Aman
Ambassador to the U.S.--Jamaluddin Jarjis
Ambassador to the UN--Hamidon Ali

Malaysia maintains an embassy in the U.S. at 3516 International Court NW, Washington, DC 20008, tel. (202) 572-9700; a Consulate General at 550 South Hope Street, Suite 400, Los Angeles, CA 90071, tel. (213) 892-1238; and a Consulate General at 313 East 43rd Street, New York City, NY 10017, tel. (212) 490-2722/23.

POLITICAL CONDITIONS

Malaysia's predominant political party, the United Malays National Organization (UMNO), has held power in coalition with other parties continuously since independence in 1957. The UMNO coalition's share of the vote declined in national elections held in May 1969, after which riots broke out in Kuala Lumpur and elsewhere, mainly between Malays and ethnic Chinese. Several hundred people were killed or injured. The government declared a state of emergency and suspended all parliamentary activities.

In the years that followed, Malaysia undertook several initiatives that became integral parts of its socioeconomic model. The New Economic Policy (NEP), launched in 1971, contained a series of affirmative action policies designed to benefit Malays and certain indigenous groups (together known as Bumiputras or "sons of the soil"). The constitution was amended to limit dissent against the specially-protected and sensitive portions of the constitution pertaining to the social contract. The government identified intercommunal harmony as one of its official goals. The previous alliance of communally based parties was replaced with a broader coalition--the Barisan Nasional (BN) or National Front. The BN won large majorities in the 1974 federal and state elections.

Mahathir Mohamad was Prime Minister between 1981 and 2003, leading UMNO and BN to successive election victories. Mahathir emphasized economic development during his tenure, in particular the export sector, as well as large-scale infrastructure projects. Mahathir attributed the success of the Asian tiger economies to the "Asian values" of its people, which he believed were superior to those of the West. Mahathir sharply criticized the International Monetary Fund (IMF), international financiers, and Western governments during the economic and financial crisis that affected Asia in 1997-1998, and denied that the sharp downturn was due to economic or corporate mismanagement, corruption, or "crony capitalism."

The end of Mahathir's tenure was marred by a falling out with his deputy and presumed successor, Anwar Ibrahim. In September 1998, Mahathir dismissed Anwar and accused him of immoral and corrupt conduct. Although Anwar was convicted on both charges in 1999 and 2000, the trials were viewed as seriously flawed. Malaysia's Federal Court eventually freed Anwar after overturning his immoral conduct conviction in September 2004.

Mahathir stepped down as Prime Minister in October 2003 after 22 years in power, and his successor, Deputy Prime Minister Abdullah Ahmad Badawi, was sworn into office. Abdullah called elections and won an overwhelming victory in March 2004. Abdullah, an Islamic scholar, promoted the concept of "Islam Hadhari" or "civilizational Islam," emphasizing the importance of education, social harmony, and economic progress. His relationship with Mahathir eventually soured, with Mahathir expressing regret at supporting Abdullah to be his successor.

Malaysia held national elections in March 2008. UMNO and its coalition allies in the BN won a simple majority of the seats in the national parliament, but for the first time in history failed to gain the two-thirds majority necessary to amend the constitution. A loose coalition of opposition parties, called the Pakatan Rakyat or People's Alliance, led by Anwar Ibrahim, won 82 of 222 seats in parliament and took control of the state-level assemblies in five of Malaysia's 13 states. However, in February 2009 the opposition Alliance lost control of one of the states through defections of its assembly members-- several members of the opposition and two from the BN became independent, bringing the opposition strength down to 79 members and the BN to 138 members. Prime Minister Abdullah, taking responsibility for his party's poor showing in the March 2008 general election, stepped down as Prime Minister in a carefully timed transfer of power to his deputy, Mohd Najib bin Abdul Razak, in April 2009.

The Najib administration's cornerstone policy is the "1Malaysia" initiative, which emphasizes national unity amongst Malaysia's ethnically diverse population. Other initiatives include the Government Transformation Program to improve government services delivery systems; the Economic Transformation Program to provide a framework to emphasize private investment and de-emphasize public investment; and the New Economic Model (NEM), to reform the 1970s (and still current) economic policy known as the New Economic Policy.

ECONOMY

Since it became independent in 1957; Malaysia's economic record has been one of Asia's best. Real gross domestic product (GDP) grew by an average of 6.5% per year from 1957 to 2005. Performance peaked in the early 1980s through the mid-1990s, as the economy experienced sustained rapid growth averaging almost 8% annually. High levels of foreign and domestic private investment played a significant role as the economy diversified and modernized. Once heavily dependent on primary products such as rubber and tin, Malaysia today is a middle-income country with a multi-sector economy based on services and manufacturing. Malaysia is one of the world's largest exporters of semiconductor devices, electrical goods, solar panels, and information and communication technology (ICT) products.

Malaysia struggled economically during the 1997-1998 Asian financial crisis and applied several valuable lessons to its economic management strategies that contributed to the economy's resilience to the 2008-2009 global financial crisis. GDP contracted 1.7% in 2009 compared to 4.6% growth in 2008, but has since rebounded, and is expected to be around 7% in 2010. Malaysian banks are well capitalized, conservatively managed, and had no measurable exposure to the U.S. sub-prime market. The central bank maintains a conservative regulatory environment, having prohibited some of the riskier assets in vogue elsewhere. Malaysia maintains high levels of foreign exchange reserves and has relatively little external debt.

The government continues to actively manage the economy with state-owned enterprises heavily involved in the oil and gas, plantation, ship building, steel, telecommunications, utilities, automotive, mining, and other sectors. Since 1971, ethnic preferences have been given to Bumiputras (ethnic Malays and indigenous peoples) by requiring 30% Bumiputra ownership in new businesses. Prime Minister Najib's New Economic Model reform program includes changes to modify these ethnic preferences and to divest state enterprises while increasing the private sector's role in stimulating higher levels of investment and boosting GDP growth. The NEM aims to create a business environment more conducive to long-term sustained economic growth, development, and investment, with the goal of Malaysia becoming a high-income, developed nation by 2020.

Malaysia has a managed float currency exchange regime. It gives flexibility for the ringgit to adjust to global economic and financial developments and has accorded a level of stability against the currencies of Malaysia's major trading partners.

FOREIGN RELATIONS

Regional cooperation is a cornerstone of Malaysia's foreign policy. It was a founding member of the Association of Southeast Asian Nations (ASEAN).

Malaysia is an active member of the Asia Pacific Economic Cooperation (APEC) forum, the Organization of the Islamic Conference (OIC), the Non-Aligned Movement (NAM), and the United Nations.

Malaysia is a frequent contributor to UN and other peacekeeping and stabilization missions, including recent deployments to Lebanon, Timor-Leste, Philippines, Indonesia, Pakistan, Sierra Leone, Sudan, Western Sahara, Nepal, and Kosovo.

U.S.-MALAYSIAN RELATIONS

The United States and Malaysia share a diverse and expanding partnership. Economic ties are robust. The United States is Malaysia's third-largest trading partner and Malaysia is the eighteenth-largest trading partner of the United States. Annual two-way trade amounts to $33 billion. In October 2010 Malaysia joined negotiations for a Trans-Pacific Partnership free trade agreement.

The United States is the largest foreign investor in Malaysia on a cumulative basis, and was the largest source of new foreign direct investment in Malayia in 2010. American companies are particularly active in the electronics, manufacturing, and oil and gas sectors. According to Malaysian data, U.S. direct investment in the manufacturing sector in Malaysia as of year-end 2009 was $15.1 billion, with billions of dollars in additional investment in the oil and gas and financial services sectors of the economy.

The United States and Malaysia cooperate closely on security matters, including counterterrorism, maritime domain awareness, and regional stability. The relationship between the U.S. and Malaysian militaries is also strong with numerous exchanges, training, joint exercises, and visits. The U.S. and Malaysia signed a Mutual Legal Assistance Treaty (MLAT) in July 2006 during the visit to Kuala Lumpur by Secretary of State Condoleezza Rice.

The United States and Malaysia have a long history of people-to-people exchanges. Well over 100,000 Malaysians have studied in the U.S. At any one time there are over 7,000 Malaysians studying at U.S. universities. Last year approximately 130 Malaysians took part in U.S. Government-sponsored exchange programs for professional development and study. Each year, about 50 Americans travel to Malaysia under U.S. Government auspices to share their experience as visiting academics or speakers. In November 2010, the U.S. and Malaysia signed a bilateral Memorandum of Understanding on Science and Technology Cooperation.

There are approximately 1,500 alumni of the International Visitor Leadership Program (IVLP) and 2,000 from the Fulbright, Humphrey, Eisenhower, and Youth Exchange for Study (YES) programs. Prominent Malaysian alumni include federal ministers, deputy ministers, and members of parliament from both the ruling party and opposition parties. At least four current and past chief ministers (state governors) are alumni, and former Prime Minister Mahathir is an alumnus of a 1973 program. These alumni have used their educations to create a stronger Malaysian society and have built enduring understanding between Malaysia and America. Their contributions to Malaysian society will continue for many years to come.

In: Malaysia: Country Profile and U.S. Relations   ISBN: 978-1-61470-172-9
Editors: G. A. Villalobos, D. E. Segura © 2011 Nova Science Publishers, Inc.

Chapter 2

U.S.-MALAYSIA RELATIONS: IMPLICATIONS OF THE 2008 ELECTIONS[*]

Michael F. Martin

SUMMARY

This report discusses key aspects of the U.S.-Malaysia relationship (including economics and trade, counterterrorism cooperation, and defense ties) and the possible impact of Malaysia's 2008 elections on the future of the relationship.

In parliamentary elections held on March 8, 2008, the Barisan Nasional (BN), which has ruled Malaysia since independence in 1957, was struck by a "political tsunami" that saw it lose its two-thirds "supermajority" for the first time since 1969. Malaysia's major opposition parties won 82 of the 222 parliamentary seats up for election. In addition, the opposition parties won control of five of Malaysia's 13 state governments. The election results are widely seen as a vote against the current policies of the Malaysian government, which could have implications for relations with the United States.

Prior to the elections, the bilateral relationship has been generally positive and constructive, particularly in the area of trade. Malaysia is a key trading partner of the United States and is regarded as an effective and cooperative regional player in the war against terror. The United States and Malaysia also have informal defense ties including commercial

---

[*] This is an edited, reformatted and augmented version of a Congressional Research Service publication, CRS Report for Congress Order Code RL33878, dated April 3, 2008.

access to Malaysian ports and repair facilities. Despite these positive dynamics, the bilateral relationship has at times been strained. Past differences have stemmed from disagreements between Malaysia's former Prime Minister Mahathir Mohamad and the United States over such issues as the internal suppression of dissent in Malaysia, the Israeli-Palestinian conflict, Iraq, globalization, Western values, and world trade policy. Relations are perceived as having improved since Abdullah Badawi became prime minister in 2003.

After years of strong economic growth, Malaysia has become a middle income country. Much of its gain in economic prosperity has come from the export of electronics and electrical products, with the United States as its top export market. According to U.S. trade figures, Malaysia exports over $30 billion of goods each year to the United States and imports over $11 billion from the United States.

The United States and Malaysia have enjoyed a positive trade relationship over the last few years, in part because both nations favor trade and investment liberalization in Asia. Malaysia is the United States' 10th largest trading partner. Building on their common perspective of international trade, Malaysia and the United States concluded a trade and investment framework agreement in 2004 and are currently negotiating a bilateral free trade agreement. Key issues still to be resolved in the negotiations principally revolve around market access for key goods and services in both the United States and Malaysia, and intellectual property rights protection in Malaysia. In addition, the dismissal of Malaysia's chief negotiator, Trade Minister Datuk Seri Rafidah Aziz, may complicate future talks.

INTRODUCTION

U.S. relations with Malaysia have been generally positive over the last few years. Both countries share interests in maintaining regional stability, dealing with militant Islamists and separatists, developing close trade and investment relationships, securing the safety of ships passing through the strategically important Strait of Malacca, and establishing mutually beneficial military cooperation. However, efforts to negotiate a bilateral free trade agreement (FTA) appear to be stalled. In addition, Malaysia and the United States appear to have conflicting views of the future of regional economic integration in East Asia.

U.S.-Malaysia relations improved after former Prime Minister Mahathir Mohamad turned over power to his former Deputy Prime Minister Datuk Seri Abdullah Badawi on October 31, 2003, ending 22 years of rule by Mahathir.

However, an unexpectedly weak showing for Badawi's political party, the United Malays National Organization (UMNO), and its Barisan Nasional (BN) coalition partners in the March 8, 2008 parliamentary elections may have implications for U.S.-Malaysian relations.

This report provides an overview of recent political and economic developments in Malaysia, and examines implications for U.S. policy.

Malaysia In Brief

Area: 127,316 sq. miles (about the size of New Mexico)
Capital: Kuala Lumpur
Population: 27.5 million (2007)
Ethnic Groups: Bumiputeras 58% [Malay 47%, Indigenous 11%], Chinese 24%, Indian 7%, Noncitizens 7%, others 4%
Religion: Muslim, Buddhist, Confucian, Taoist, Christian, Hindu, Sikh, Baha'i
Literacy Rate: 92.5% (2006)
Life Expectancy: Female - 76.3 years; Male - 71.8 years (2006)

Sources: Malaysia Ministry of Finance, Economic Report 2007/2008.

MALAYSIA'S 2008 ELECTIONS

UMNO and its coalition partners have been in power since Malaysia's independence in 1957. In the first general election in 1959, UMNO and its coalition partners[1] received just over half the votes, but won 74 out of the 104 seats in the *Dewan Rakyat* (People's Hall), the more powerful lower house of Malaysia's parliament.[2] In every parliamentary election from 1959 to 2004,[3] an UMNO-led coalition has won at least two-thirds of the seats in parliament — with the exception of 1969, when the coalition won 95 out of 144 seats (66.0%). A two-thirds "supermajority" is important because it allows the BN to amend Malaysia's constitution without support from opposition parties. In the election of 2004, the BN won 198 out of 219, or 90.4%, of the seats.

Political "Tsunami"

The outcome of the parliamentary elections of March 8, 2008, surprised many people. A major Malaysian newspaper, *The Star*, quoted one opposition leader who compared the results to a tsunami.[4] The BN barely received half of the popular vote, and won just 140 of the 222 seats in the *Dewan Rakyat* — eight seats less than it needed to retain a "supermajority." The biggest losers among the BN members were:

- UMNO, which saw its seats decline from 109 to 79;
- The Malaysian Chinese Association (MCA), which dropped from 31 to 15 seats; and
- The Malaysian People's Movement Party (*Parti Gerakan Rakyat Malaysia*, or Gerakan), which held onto only 2 of its 10 seats in the *Dewan Rakyat*.

Most commentators stated the 2008 elections were the BN's worst results since 1959. The main opposition parties — the Democratic Action Party (DAP), the Islamic Party of Malaysia (*Parti Islam SeMalaysia*, or PAS), and the People's Justice Party (*Parti Keadilan Rakyat*, or PKR) — all increased their number of seats in the parliament. The PKR experienced the greatest rise — jumping from just one to 31 seats. The DAP and PAS both increased their seats on the *Dewan Rakyat* by 16 seats, for a total of 28 and 23, respectively. Altogether, Malaysia's opposition parties received 46.8% of the popular vote, and won 82 out of the 222 seats on the *Dewan Rakyat*.

The BN's weakness was also reflected in the results of the 12 concurrent state elections.[5] Opposition parties took control of five of the 13 Malaysian states, including surprise victories in Kedah, Penang, and Selangor. The PAS retained its control over the state of Kelantan and the DAP leads a small opposition majority in the state of Perak. Among the seven contested states in which the BN retained control, the opposition gained seats in all but two states — Perlis and Sabah.

There are differing opinions on why the BN lost so much of its support, and the opposition parties gained so much support. Some commentators maintain that Badawi was responsible because he had failed to make adequate reforms within the BN and the government . Others stated that economic factors, and in particular rising income disparities and inflation, had led voters to switch from the BN to the opposition parties. Another group of political observers saw the election results as evidence that Malaysia's ethnicity-based political system was obsolete and no longer a reliable base of power for the BN.

Implications of the Elections

In the immediate aftermath of the elections, ex-prime minister Mahathir suggested Badawi should consider resigning.[6] While Badawi did not resign, he did reorganize his cabinet, reducing the number of ministers (from 90 to 70) and removing several long-standing members. According to Badawi, half of the members of the cabinet announced on March 18, 2008, were "new faces."[7] Among the people removed from the cabinet was Datuk Seri Rafidah Aziz, who had held the position of Minister of International Trade and Industry for over 20 years. Aziz has been an important figure in U.S.-Malaysian trade relations. It is unclear what impact, if any, the new cabinet will have on Malaysia's policies.

The dramatic drop in support for two of Malaysia's ethnically-based political parties — the MCA and the Malaysian Indian Congress (MIC) — has also led to calls for political changes. Gerakan party chief Datuk Chang Ko Youn, who lost his seat in the parliament to a DAP candidate, has suggested that BN member parties should consider eliminating ethnic restrictions on party membership as a first step to the formation of a single party.[8] However, MIC president Seri S. Samy Vellu, who also lost his bid for reelection to the parliament to an opposition candidate, rejected Chang's suggestion, saying "such an action will dilute the rights of the Indian community."[9] Some commentators have suggested that the shift in Chinese and Indian support to opposition party candidates reflects a growing sense among Malaysia's influential ethnic minorities that the BN no longer adequate reflects their interests. Others attribute the desertion of the BN by Malaysia's Chinese and Indian to economic issues, such as food price inflation and rising income disparities.

The strengthening of opposition party power in the *Dewan Rakyat* and in state governments is also expected to restrict the power of Badawi and the BN to implement changes in policy. The loss of a supermajority in the *Dewan Rakyat* is considered by some a psychological and political blow to the BN, which has ruled virtually unchallenged in Malaysia since independence. There is discussion that the election results may be the first sign that politics in Malaysia are starting the process of transformation into a two-party, non-ethnic system, and possibly a more truly democratic process.

In addition, opposition control of five of Malaysia's 13 states may also curtail Badawi's power. For example, the new state government in Penang has already announced that it will no longer abide by the BN's long-standing "New Economic Policy" that grants preferential treatment to Malaysia's *bumiputera*.[10] However, a past judicial tradition of broadly interpreting the federal government's power under Malaysia's constitution may mitigate the opposition's ability to use the state governments to exert power or influence.

A final concern raised by the BN's weak showing in the 2008 is the potential for social unrest and governmental policy change. The last time the BN (or its predecessors) did as poorly in a parliamentary election was in 1969. Following the 1969 elections, there were violent ethnic riots in Malaysia between May and July (precipitated by the "May 13 Incident" in Kuala Lumpur) during which approximately 200 people were killed. Following the riots of 1969, the BN announced a series of economic reforms, known as the "New Economic Policy" (NEP). The events of 1969 are discussed in more detail below. However, in the weeks following the election, there has been virtually no violence or ethnic unrest in Malaysia.

For U.S.-Malaysia relations, the 2008 elections will have little direct or immediate impact, with the possible exception of the removal of Aziz as Minister of International Trade and Industry. Aziz has been Malaysia's chief negotiator during the U.S.-Malaysia free trade agreement (FTA) talks. Her departure implies a loss of "institutional knowledge" for the Malaysian negotiation team. Her replacement, Tan Sri Muhyiddin Yassin, was Minister of Agriculture and Agro-based Industry in the previous cabinet.

MALAYSIA'S POLITICAL DYNAMICS

Many of the political cleavages of Malaysian society, which continue to have relevance to today's political dynamics, find their root in Malaysia's colonial past. Malaysia inherited a diverse demographic mix from the British. Through the importation of labor, the British added ethnic Chinese and Indians to the Malay and other indigenous populations of peninsular Malaya, Sabah, and Sarawak. The demographic composition of Sabah and Sarawak includes a higher percentage of indigenous groups, such as the Iban. Together the Malay and indigenous population — collectively known as the *bumiputeras* — comprise about 58% of the population compared to 24% for the Chinese and 7% for the Indians. Traditionally, ethnic Chinese and Indians have controlled a disproportionately greater share of the nation's wealth than bumiputeras.

Malaysia has a complex history of inter-communal politics. A British plan after World War II to create the Malaysian Union that incorporated all of the Malayan territories except Singapore would have provided for common citizenship regardless of ethnicity. Concerns among the Malays that they could not compete with the more commercially-minded Chinese led to the creation of UMNO — a conservative, Malay nationalist organization that later reformed itself into a political party. Negotiations between the British and UMNO led to the creation of the Federation of Malaya in 1948, which included Singapore and provided special rights for the bumiputeras and Malaysia's sultans. Sabah and Sarawak joined the Federation to form Malaysia later in 1963, while Singapore left the Federation in 1965. At independence in 1957, there was an understanding that Malays would exert a dominant position in political life in Malaya, while ethnic Chinese and Indians would be given citizenship and allowed to continue their role in the economy.[11]

This accommodation between Malaysia's ethnic groups has not always been tranquil. Between 1948 and 1960, the Communist Party of Malaysia, which was largely comprised of ethnic Chinese, waged a guerilla war against the British. This came to be known as the "Malayan Emergency."[12] The Internal Security Act (ISA), which continues to be used to suppress groups that threaten the regime, originally was put in place by the British to combat "communist subversion." The Special Branch, which Malaysia inherited from the British, continues to act as the primary intelligence and security unit under the Royal Malaysian Police. During the "Emergency," Malays generally sided with the British against the communists whose ranks were drawn largely from the Chinese community. By the mid-1950s, the insurrection had collapsed.

Added to this history of inter-communal strife were the riots of May to July 1969 in which reportedly 196 were killed. Most of those killed were ethnic Chinese. Rioting began on May 13, three days after the Alliance Party, a predecessor to the BN, failed to win two-thirds of the seats in the *Dewan Rakyat*, and lost control of Selangor and Perak. Much like the results of the 2008 elections, one of the main losers in the 1969 elections was MCA, which lost 14 of its 27 seats in the *Dewan Rakyat*. Because of the rioting, elections to be held in Sabah and Sarawak were suspended and a state of emergency was declared.[13]

Partly in response to the 1969 riots, the New Economic Policy (NEP) was instituted in 1971. NEP provided preferential treatment for the bumiputera majority via a kind of quota system in order to increase their share of the economic wealth of the country. The New Development Policy (NDP) replaced the NEP in 1990. The NDP retained NEP goals, such as 30%

bumiputera control of corporate assets. Prime Minister Mahathir's subsequent *Vision 2020* policy had similar elements, but was more inclusive and attempted to do more to foster national ethnic unity.[14]

The BN appears to be relying on an expanding economy to be able to disproportionately favor bumiputeras, while not undermining its economic appeal to Malaysia's Chinese and Indian population. In this way, Malaysia's social harmony — and support for the BN — may be linked to economic growth. For this reason, periods of economic stagnation could carry the prospect of eroding the delicate balance between ethnic groups in Malaysia and undermining support for the BN.

Internal Politics

Malaysia is a Constitutional Monarchy, but of an unusual kind, whose structure includes 13 states and three federal territories. Every five years, the nine hereditary Sultans elect one from among their group to be the Yang di Pertuan Agong, a traditional title equating to a King. The Agong exercises limited authority and acts on the advice of the Prime Minister, Parliament and the Cabinet. The Prime Minister is the head of the Federal Government, which has 25 ministries. Out of a total of 13 states four are ruled by State Governors appointed by the Federal Government. In the nine other states, the hereditary Sultan fulfills this function. Each state has a state legislature. The lower house of Malaysia's Parliament, the *Dewan Rakyat*, has 222 members elected for terms not to exceed five years. The upper house, the *Dewan Negara*, has 70 members — 44 members appointed by the King and 26 elected members with two from each state.

Malaysia is an "ambiguous, mixed"[15] or "semi"[16] democracy that has both democratic and authoritarian elements. The constitution is largely democratic and provides for regular elections that are responsive to the electorate. The government is based on a parliamentary system and the judiciary is designed to be independent. Despite this democratic structure, authoritarian control limits the ability of the opposition to defeat the ruling coalition at the polls.[17]

Prime Minister Badawi heads the United Malays National Organization (UMNO), the key party in the BN. The BN also includes the Malaysian Chinese Association (MCA), the Malaysian Indian Congress (MIC), the *Parti Gerakan Rakyat Malaysia* (Malaysian People's Movement Party, or Gerakan), and a number of smaller political parties. The opposition is led by the Pan-Malaysian Islamic Party (*Parti Islam Se-Malaysia*, or PAS), the People's

Justice Party (Parti Keadilan Rakyat, or PKR), and the Democratic Action Party (DAP). In 1999, PAS, DAP, PKR, and Malaysian People's Party (*Parti Rakyat Malaysia*, or PRM) formed an opposition alliance known as the *Barisan Alternatif* (Alternative Front), but the alliance fragmented in 2001 following the withdrawal of the DAP. For the 2008 elections, DAP, PAS, and the PKR formed an alliance called the *Barisan Rakyat* (People's Front) with a number of smaller parties.

UMNO is the most influential party in Malaysia today and represents the interests of the mostly Sunni Malays. The Malaysian administration, under both Mahathir and Badawi, has promoted a moderate form of Islam — *Islam Hadhari* (see below) — under a secular polity while opposing the rise of Islamic extremists whose policies are more closely associated with PAS.[18] The ruling BN, under Mahathir's leadership, used the power of the state, including the ISA, to thwart political gains by PAS, which advocates a more conservative view of Islam. PAS's influence is traditionally found in the northeast states of Kelantan and Terengganu.[19]

The transition from Mahathir to Badawi was consolidated in the March 21, 2004 elections that expanded the ruling BN's hold on parliament from 77% to 90% of the seats. The BN also increased its share of votes from 57% to 64%.[20] Following the 2004 elections, the government's coalition controlled 11 of 12 state governments. The election was viewed by observers as a vote of confidence by Malaysians in Badawi's relatively moderate form of Islamic practice as opposed to the hard-line approach of PAS.[21] The PAS, which offered a more Islamist agenda, lost voter confidence, including in its area of traditional support in northeast peninsular Malaya.[22]

The political transition from Mahathir to Badawi led to an improvement of U.S.- Malaysian relations. Some think Badawi, who was first elected to Parliament in 1978, is attempting to strike a balance between providing continuity of leadership to produce stability, and meeting expectations for a more open and consultative style of government. Badawi pledged to work with the BN to realize the policy goals articulated in *Vision 2020*.[23] It is thought that Badawi's political legitimacy will at least in part be dependent on his ability to deliver sound economic growth and to counter the perceived rise of Islamic extremism in Malaysia.[24] Badawi's respected religious background[25] has helped him counter the rising popularity of PAS and the forces of Islamic extremism.

However, Badawi's government has been beset by division within UMNO. In part, these are based on differences between former Prime Minister Mahathir Muhammad and Prime Minister Badawi. More recently, now ex-

Minister Aziz has supposedly used her leadership of the Wanita Umno, UMNO's main women's organization, in an attempt to influence government and party policies. It is thought that party divisions led Badawi to call for the early general elections of 2008 in hopes of securing a fresh mandate and reinforcing his position within his party.[26] The outcome of the elections was clearly contrary to his hopes.

Islam Hadhari

Under Badawi's leadership, Malaysia has been developing a concept, *Islam Hadhari*, that seeks to promote a moderate or progressive view of Islamic civilization.[27] Badawi has stated that "we are responsible for ensuring that the culture of extremism and violent acts in the name of Islam does not happen in Malaysia."[28]

Some observers believe that *Islam Hadhari* could promote a view of Islam that encourages and emphasizes development, social justice and tolerance.[29] Increasing attention appears to be focused on the role that moderate Islamic ideology and moderate Islamic states can play in countering the forces of Islamic extremism within the region and beyond. However, some analysts are concerned about what they see as an "increasing Islamisation trend in Malaysia" and that "a more conservative form of Islam is emerging" in Malaysia despite government efforts through *Islam Hadhari* to "pave the way for the development of Malaysia as a bastion of Islamic moderation."[30]

MALAYSIA'S INTERNATIONAL RELATIONS

Malaysia has been playing an active role in international organizations both in its region and beyond. Besides Asia Pacific Economic Cooperation (APEC), ASEAN, and the World Trade organization (WTO), Malaysia is also a member of the Asian Development Bank (ADB), the Islamic Development Bank, the Non-Aligned Movement (NAM), Organization of Islamic Conference (OIC), the United Nations, and the World Bank. In 2006, Malaysia chaired ASEAN, the Organization of Islamic Conference (OIC), and the Non-Aligned Movement (NAM). Malaysia has been an active contributor to international peacekeeping, including most recently in East Timor. It also sent personnel to assist the Aceh Monitoring Mission in Indonesia in 2005 and

2006. Malaysia has also been seeking to facilitate negotiations between the government of the Philippines and the Moro Islamic Liberation Front.[31]

Regional Relations

Malaysia has placed much emphasis on regional cooperation despite its differences with certain regional states. In the past, Malaysia and the Philippines have differed over the Philippines' claim to parts of Sabah. Indonesia and Malaysia came into conflict as a result of Indonesian military raids over the border in Borneo in 1963. These were part of its policy of confrontasi and repelled by Malaysian and Commonwealth forces. Malaysia remains a member in the Five Power Defense Arrangements along with Australia, New Zealand, the United Kingdom, and Singapore, which has its roots in Malaysia's colonial past.

Malaysia has significant interest in the hydrocarbon potential of the South China Sea. In the past, this has put Malaysia in conflict with Brunei over the Baram Delta off the coast of Sabah and Sarawak. In July 2002, independent U.S. contractor Murphy Oil, working for Malaysia's state oil company Petronas, discovered the Kikeh field, which is estimated to hold 700 million barrels of oil.[32] This represents 21% of Malaysia's current reserves, which are projected to run out in 15 years.[33] Malaysia, China, the Philippines, and Vietnam have conflicting claims over the Spratly Islands and the South China Sea. Though continuing, this conflict has been less contentious in recent years than it was in the 1990s.

Malaysia was a founding member of ASEAN in 1967 and in the 1990s was a strong advocate for expanding ASEAN to include Burma, Laos, and Vietnam. More recently, Malaysia has sought a more influential role in ASEAN and Southeast Asia, particularly with respect to trade issues. Malaysia hosted the East Asian Summit in Kuala Lumpur in December 2005 as part of its efforts to transform ASEAN into a more integrated regional association.[34] Malaysia also promoted the drafting of the new ASEAN Charter and is one of the five members to ratify the new agreement.[35] In addition, Malaysia has supported efforts to form closer trade relations with nations outside of ASEAN via the "ASEAN+3" and "ASEAN+6" models. However, Malaysia's relatively small size and a lack of consensus in ASEAN to follow a Malaysian lead place limits on the extent to which Malaysia can assume a leadership role within ASEAN and the region.

Malaysia-China Relations

The attitudes of Malaysia (and other ASEAN states) towards China have undergone a significant shift over the past two decades.[36] Relations with China were once characterized by much suspicion. More recently, Malaysia has viewed China as both a major competitor and a major trading partner. There are some indications that Malaysia has attempted to maintain the value of its currency, the ringit, in line with the value of China's currency, the renminbi, to protect its competitive position in key commodity markets.

Malaysia normalized relations with China in 1974, but has maintained close economic and trade relations with Taiwan. Over 2,000 Taiwanese companies have invested in Malaysia. In 2007, while China was Malaysia's 4th largest trading partner, Taiwan was its 7th largest trading partner. Hong Kong, a special administrative region of China, was Malaysia's 8th largest trading partner in 2007.

In recent years, issues of economic competition and cooperation have been more of a concern to ASEAN states than security concerns.[37] China currently is said to be thought of "as more of an opportunity with concomitant challenges, rather than as a threat" as it was as recently as 1999, when China fortified Mischief Reef in the South China Sea which it had occupied in 1994.[38] To assert its claims to the South China Sea, Malaysia constructed a concrete building on Investigator Shoal in the Spratlys in 1998. ASEAN states' perceptions could change again should China more actively reassert its claims in the South China Sea or go to war over Taiwan.[39]

Malaysia-Indonesia Relations

Relations between Malaysia and Indonesia have at times been tense. Among the top issues between the two nations are differences over Malaysian policies towards illegal Indonesian workers and a maritime dispute off Borneo which has implications for control of valuable energy resources. The presence of thousands of illegal Indonesian workers in Malaysia that have supposedly displaced many of Malaysia's Indian workers may have contributed to Malaysia's Indian population deserting UMNO and the BN in the 2008 elections.[40] Many undocumented Indonesians working in Malaysia were pressed to leave Malaysia in late 2004 and early 2005.[41] There are also allegations of the human trafficking of Indonesian women and children to Malaysia for commercial sexual exploitation.[42]

Malaysia also awarded an oil concession to Royal Dutch Shell in 2005 in the waters off Sabah in northeastern Borneo that are also claimed by Indonesia. The conflict escalated to the point that both nations sent naval ships to assert their claims before diplomacy eased tensions.[43] Malaysia agreed to participate in the monitoring of the peace treaty signed in August 2005 between Indonesia and Gerakan Aceh Merdeka (GAM) along with the international monitoring team led by the European Union.[44] Malaysia has also called for ASEAN states to discuss defense issues as well as foreign and economic policy.[45]

Illegal forest fires in Sumatra in August 2005 led Malaysia to close schools, as well as Malaysia's largest seaport, and declare a state of emergency in Kuala Selangor and Port Kelang as smoke severely limited visibility and created a significant health risk.[46] The Indonesian government reportedly placed the blame for the fires on 10 logging companies, of which 8 were Malaysian-owned.[47] Given that illegal burning of forests in Indonesia has led to dangerous smoke pollution in Malaysia before, some observers have speculated that more must be done to put in place legal frameworks to control trans-border pollution.[48] An estimated 70% of all logging in Indonesia is illegal.[49]

Badawi met with his Indonesian counterpart, President H. Susilo Bambang Yudhoyono, on January 11, 2008, in Putrajaya, Malaysia, as part of the "annual consultations" between the two countries. Their discussions focused on the land and maritime border issues, bilateral defense cooperation, Indonesian migrant workers in Malaysia, illegal logging, and bilateral economic cooperation.

Other Bilateral Relations

Malaysia's border with Thailand has been a source of friction in their bilateral relationship. Thailand's southern provinces are Muslim majority areas where separatist violence has been increasing. Malaysia agreed to work with Thailand under a Joint Development Strategy for border areas to develop the economy and living conditions of people in the border region. Badawi has highlighted the need to address poverty as a means of alleviating the conflict in Southern Thailand.[50]

Malaysia's relations with neighboring Singapore have been termed "bumpy" since Singapore's independence in 1965. The "bumpiness" of the relationship emerges from several factors, including ethnic tensions, economic and trade interdependency, and common security concerns.[51] Singapore is a largely Chinese city-state with a large Malay minority; Malaysia is a largely Malay nation with a large Chinese minority. Economic conditions force Singapore to rely on Malaysia for many resources, including water and labor. At the same time, Malaysia relies on Singapore for capital investments and trade-related business opportunities, including the reexport of many Malaysian goods. Finally, both nations are reliant on the flow of shipments through the Strait of Malacca. In addition to the Five Power Defense Arrangement, Malaysia and Singapore also have established coordinated naval patrols with Indonesia to protect freight shipments in the region. According to Singapore's minister of foreign affairs, George Yeo, the results of the 2008 elections should not affect bilateral relations.[52]

MALAYSIA'S ECONOMY AND FOREIGN TRADE

Malaysia is a relatively mature industrialized nation, whose economy relies on both domestic forces (personal consumption and private investment) and external trade for its growth and development. Following a short, severe recession in 1998 and a mild turndown in 2001,[53] Malaysia's real gross domestic product (GDP) has grown between 5% and 6% per year for the past five years. The current official government estimate has its real GDP increasing 6.0% in 2007 and projecting 6.0%- 6.5% growth in 2008 (see **Table 1**). Malaysia's central bank, Bank Negara Malaysia, projected 2008 GDP growth of 5.0%-6.0% two weeks after the parliamentary elections, citing "turbulent global financial markets and slowing U.S. growth" as reasons for its less optimistic forecast.[54]

Malaysia's GDP and average per capita income classify it as a middle income country according the World Bank's system, comparable to Mexico and Russia.[55] At official exchange rates, the per capita income in 2007 was $5,740, but its purchasing power parity value was estimated at $13,289.

Since the 2001 economic downturn, Malaysia's economic growth has relied on a combination of strong domestic demand and continued export growth. In 2007, the main sources of real GDP growth were (in order): domestic consumption, public consumption, public investment, and private investment. Because imports grew more rapidly than exports, 6.2% compared to 4.1%, external trade actually lowered economic expansion in 2007. Government forecasts project private investment will play a greater role in economic growth in 2008, surpassing both public investment and public consumption.

Another indication of the maturation of Malaysia's economy is its sectoral balance (see Table 2). While agriculture and manufacturing continue to play an important role in Malaysia's economy, the nation's GDP mainly comes from the service sectors. The sectoral structure of Malaysia's economy is more akin to those of South Korea and Thailand than Indonesia, the Philippines and Vietnam.

Table 1. Selected Indicators for the Malaysian Economy

	2006	2007 (est.)	2008 (proj.)
Real GDP Growth	5.9%	6.0%	6.0- 6.5%
Nominal GDP (billion ringgits)	572.555	641.499	681.7
Nominal GDP ($ billion)	148.940	161.843	n.a.
Nominal GDP per Capita ($)	5,383	5,740	n.a.
GDP per Capita - purchasing power parity.[a] ($)	11,663	13,289	14,206
Inflation Rate - CPI	3.6%	2.0%	2.5 - 3.0%
Inflation Rate - PPI	6.8%	6.8%	n.a.
Unemployment Rate	3.3%	3.3%	n.a.
Exports ($ billion; fob)	160.845	176.311	188.3
Imports ($ billion; cif)	131.223	147.065	159.1
Exchange rate (ringgits per U.S. dollar)	3.678	3.447	n.a.

Source: Malaysia's Ministry of Finance; World Trade Atlas; and CRS calculations.

[a] Purchasing power parity estimates of per capita GDP attempt to revalue official GDP figures by comparing the relative costs of a select group of goods in each nation and then recalculating per capita GDP to reflect the relative purchasing power in each nation.

Although agriculture provides a relatively small portion of Malaysia's GDP, it plays an important role in the nation's overall economy. One out of every three Malaysians live in rural areas. Approximately one out of every eight workers in Malaysia are employed in agriculture, animal husbandry, fishing, or forestry. Rice and palm oil are two crops of particular importance to Malaysia, the former for political reasons because many Malaysian farmers are reliant on rice for their livelihood and are opposed to the import of rice. The latter is important for economic reasons, as palm oil is a traditional major export crop for Malaysia.

Table 2. Share of GDP by Sector: 2000, 2006-2008

Sector	2000	2006	2007 (est.)	2008 (proj.)
Agriculture	9.4%	7.9%	7.7%	7.5%
Construction	3.6%	3.1%	3.0%	3.0%
Manufacturing	30.0%	31.1%	30.3%	29.6%
Mining	7.2%	8.8%	8.6%	8.4%
Services	54.3%	51.8%	53.2%	54.3%
Adjustments	0.0%	-2.7%	-2.8%	-2.8%

Source: Department of Statistics, Malaysia.

Malaysia's manufacturing sector accounts for nearly a third of the nation's GDP, employs about 30% of its workers, and accounts for over 80% of its export earnings. It is dominated by the production of automobiles, and electrical and electronic products.

Malaysia is a regional leader in the production of automobiles, automotive components and parts. Its two major automobile manufacturers, Proton and Perodua, export their vehicles to over 40 countries, and Malaysia's leading motorcycle manufacturer, Modenas, exports to markets around the world, including Argentina, Greece, Iran, Malta, Mauritius, Singapore, Turkey, and Vietnam. Malaysia's automotive industry benefits from Malaysia's tariff and non-tariff trade restrictions on the import of automobiles, motorcycles, and components and parts for automobiles and motorcycles.

The electrical and electronics (E&E) industry of Malaysia is a world-leader in the production of semiconductors and the assembly of E&E products, much of which is done under contract for leading international electronics companies. Approximately half of Malaysia's export earnings come from the E&E industry. However, over half of Malaysia's imports are raw materials, components, equipment, and capital goods to be used by its E&E manufacturers. As a result, the nation's economy is somewhat dependent on the global demand for electrical and electronic products.

Malaysia's service sector is highly diversified, providing services for both the domestic and external segments of the economy. The service sector provides over 54% of the nation's GDP and more than half of its employment. Following the Asian financial crisis in 1997, Malaysia placed severe restriction on foreign participation in some service sectors, including financial services. Over the last five years, Malaysia has gradually loosened those restrictions, but access to Malaysia's financial markets is still very limited to foreign companies.

Foreign trade was a major driver of Malaysia's economic growth in the past and continues to be important for its overall economic health. According to official figures, Malaysia's total trade exceeded 1 trillion ringgits for the first time in 2006. Over the last six years, Malaysia's exports increased 81.0% in value, while its imports rose by 80.2% (see Table 3). Malaysia runs a balance of trade surplus of about $30 billion per year.

Table 3. Malaysia's Exports, Imports and Merchandise Trade Balance, 2001-2007
(billion ringgits and U.S. dollars)

Year	Exports	Imports	Trade Balance
2001	334.3 (88.2)	280.2 (73.866)	54.0 (14.336)
2002	357.4 (93.370)	303.1 (79.870)	54.3 (13.500)
2003	397.9 (100.113)	316.5 (80.093)	81.4 (20.020)
2004	480.7 (125.857)	400.1 (105.297)	80.7 (20.560)
2005	533.8 (140.979)	434.0 (114.626)	99.8 (26.353)
2006	589.0 (160.845)	480.8 (131.223)	108.2 (29.622)
2007	605.2 (176.311)	504.8 (147.065)	100.4 (29.246)

Sources: Ministry of Statistics, Malaysia and Global Trade Atlas.

According to Malaysia's trade statistics, the United States was and continues to be its largest export market (see Table 4). In 2007, 15.6% of Malaysia's exports went to the United States, down from 18.8% in 2006. With the exception of the Netherlands and the United States, all of Malaysia's top 10 export markets are in the Asia-Pacific, indicating a regional export focus.

Japan is historically the largest supplier of Malaysia's imports, but the United States was a close second in 2006 (see Table 5). Outside of Germany and the United States, all of Malaysia's leading suppliers of imports are in Asia, more evidence of its regional trade focus.

Of Malaysia's largest trading partners, China, Japan, South Korea, and Taiwan have a bilateral merchandise trade surplus. Every other nation has a bilateral trade deficit, with the United States running the largest bilateral trade deficit. According to Malaysia's trade figures, both Malaysia's exports to the United States and its imports from the United States declined in 2007, by 14.6% and 9.1% respectively.

**Table 4. Malaysia's Top 10 Export Markets
(billion ringgits)**

Partner	2006	2007
Total Exports	589.0	605.2
United States	110.6	94.5
Singapore	90.8	88.5
Japan	52.2	55.2
China	42.7	53.0
Thailand	31.2	30.0
Hong Kong	29.1	28.0
Netherlands	21.4	23.6
South Korea	21.3	23.0
Australia	16.7	20.4
India	18.8	20.2

Source: Ministry of International Trade and Industry, Malaysia.

**Table 5. Malaysia's Imports by Top 10 Trading Partners
(billion ringgits)**

Partner	2006	2007
Total Imports	480.8	504.8
Japan	63.6	65.5
China	58.2	64.9
Singapore	56.2	58.0
United States	60.2	54.7
Taiwan	26.2	28.7
Thailand	26.3	27.0
South Korea	25.9	24.9
Germany	21.1	23.4
Indonesia	18.2	21.4
Hong Kong	12.7	14.7

Source: Ministry of International Trade and Industry, Malaysia.

Malaysia's Current Economic Policies

The current goals for Malaysia's economic policies are to continue its strong economic growth, maintain full employment, reduce inflationary pressures, and lower the fiscal deficit. In addition, as part of its larger policy of

Islam Hadhari, the government seeks to reduce poverty, improve living standards, and reduce income and wealth inequality between the nation's various ethnic groups. In particular, there is concern about the income and wealth differential between the bumiputera and the ethnic Chinese and Indian of Malaysia.

For the period 2006 to 2010, the Malaysian government has established a set of objectives to achieve its overall economic goals as part of its Ninth Malaysia Plan.[56] First, it will attempt to move its production into higher value-added activities by greater investment in education. Second, Malaysia seeks to improve the quality of the Malaysian work force by promoting the values of *Islam Hadahari* and improving the quality of Malaysia's educational system. Third, the government will address persistent sources of both regional and ethnic economic inequality. Fourth, Malaysia will seek to eliminate poverty by 2010 and continue to improve living standards. Fifth, in order to facilitate the achievement of the preceding objectives, the Malaysia government will strengthen the quality of its government agencies.

The key macroeconomic policies for the Ninth Malaysia Plan emphasize continued growth by increasing the role of Malaysia's private sector and by attracting foreign direct investment (FDI), especially in higher value-added activities. In addition, the government will attempt to keep inflation under control. Also, there is the explicit objective of reducing the federal fiscal deficit from 3.8% of GDP in 2005 to 3.4% of GDP in 2010. Finally, having ended the peg of the ringgit to the U.S. dollar on July 21, 2005, Malaysia's central bank, the Bank Negara Malaysia, has officially adopted a managed float of the ringgit against several foreign currencies.[57] However, there is some evidence that Malaysia's de facto exchange rate policy is to maintain the value of the ringgit relatively constant when compared to the value of China's renminbi.[58]

Malaysia's stated foreign trade policy for the next five years will continue to support trade and investment liberalization. Malaysia had projected the value of total trade (imports plus exports) will exceed 1 trillion ringgits ($286 billion) by 2010, but achieved that figure in 2006 and 2007. The government sees the formation of the proposed ASEAN Free Trade Area (AFTA), the trade liberalization and facilitation efforts of the Asia-Pacific Economic Cooperation (APEC), and the current efforts by the World Trade Organization (WTO) for greater liberalization of trade in goods and services as being consistent with its overall trade policy. In particular, Malaysia strongly supports ASEAN's discussions with China, Japan, and South Korea — the so-called "ASEAN+3" — about the possibility of forming an East Asian economic community. The successful conclusion of a free trade agreement with the United States would also be viewed as being consistent with its current trade policy.

U.S.-Malaysia Bilateral Trade

In general, trade relations between the United States and Malaysia are dominated by the outsourcing of the production of machinery, and electronic and electrical products by multinational corporations with operations within the United States and Malaysia. This trade pattern is revealed by the cross-shipment of similarly categorized goods to and from Malaysia, as well as the sector structure of U.S. foreign direct investment (FDI) in Malaysia. From 2001 to 2006, Malaysia's exports to the United States grew substantially, regardless of which nation's trade statistics are used, but then noticeably declined in 2007 (see Table 6). However, U.S. exports to Malaysia have not experienced similar growth. As a result, the U.S. bilateral trade deficit with Malaysia increased between 2001 and 2007 — up $9.2 billion according to the United States and $5.6 billion according to Malaysia.

Table 6. U.S.-Malaysia Bilateral Trade Flows, 2001-2006
(Billion dollars)

	2001	2002	2003	2004	2005	2006	2007
U.S. Figures							
Exports to Malaysia	9.4	10.3	10.9	10.9	10.5	12.6	11.7
% of Total Exports	1.3	1.5	1.5	1.3	1.2	1.2	1.0
Imports from Malaysia	22.3	24.0	25.4	28.2	33.7	36.5	32.8
% of Total Imports	2.0	2.1	2.0	1.9	2.0	2.0	1.7
	2001	2002	2003	2004	2005	2006	2007
Malaysian Figures							
Exports to U.S.	17.8	18.8	17.8	23.6	27.7	30.2	27.5
% of Total Exports	20.2	20.2	17.8	18.7	19.7	18.8	15.6
Imports from U.S.	11.8	13.1	12.2	15.2	14.8	16.4	15.9
% of Total Imports	16.0	16.4	15.2	14.5	12.9	12.5	10.8

Source: Global Trade Atlas.

In addition, the relative importance of each other as a trading partner has declined since 2001. From Malaysia's perspective, the United States purchased 20.2% of its exports in 2001, but only 15.6 of its exports in 2007. Similarly, the United States provided Malaysia with 16.0% of its imports in 2001, but just 10.8% of its imports in 2007. For the United States, Malaysia was the supplier of 2.0% of its imports in 2001 and 1.7% in 2007, and was the buyer of 1.3% of its exports in 2001 and 1.0% of its exports in 2007.

Table 7 lists the top by categories of goods traded between Malaysia and the United States in 2007, according to U.S. trade data. The data reveals considerable reciprocal trade in machinery (HS84), electrical machinery (HS85); over three-quarters of bilateral trade in 2007 was in these two types of commodities. Much of this cross trade was due to outward processing of electronic and electrical products in Malaysia by major U.S. companies.

Table 7. Top Five U.S. Exports to and Imports from Malaysia, 2007 (in million dollars)

Exports		Imports	
Commodity	Value	Commodity	Value
Electrical Machinery	6,320.6	Machinery (84)	14,500.4
Machinery (84)	1,709.7	Electrical Machinery (85)	10,941.4
Optical & Medical Instruments (90)	691.4	Optical & Medical Instruments (90)	957.0
Iron & Steel	411.7	Rubber (40)	839.5
Aircraft (98)	320.2	Furniture & Bedding	829.7

In the bilateral exchange of machinery in 2007, the United States and Malaysia were shipping back and forth mostly computers and related equipment (HS8471) and parts and accessories for office equipment (HS8473). In the exchange of electronics and electrical products, the United States exports were mostly integrated circuits and microassemblies (HS8542) and its imports were primarily telephones and telephone parts (HS8517), as well as a significant amount of integrated circuits and microassemblies (HS8542).

Since 2000, the United States has consistently been among the leading sources of foreign direct investment (FDI) in Malaysia, along with Hong Kong, Japan, and Singapore. In 2007, the United States invested 3.0 billion ringgits ($870 million) in Malaysia, which was 17.3% of Malaysia's total inward FDI for the year.[59] The United States was Malaysia's fourth largest source of FDI in 2007, after (in order): Japan (6.5 billion ringgits), Germany (3.7 billion ringgits), and Iran (3.1 billion ringgits). The cumulative value of U.S. FDI in Malaysia is over $20 billion, with much of it being invested in electronics and electrical manufacturing, as well as the petrochemical industry.

MALAYSIA AND U.S. TRADE RELATIONS

Malaysia and the United States currently hold similar positions on international trade relations in general, but occasionally differ on specific issues. Both nations support the general concept of trade and investment liberalization and facilitation. Also, both are actively pursuing trade and investment liberalization via multilateral and bilateral fora. However, on specific issues, there are differences between the United States and Malaysia on the goals and means of obtaining those goals. As a result, the two nations sometimes share the same view on trade issues, and sometimes have different, and even, opposing views.

Since Malaysia and the United States are members of the World Trade Organization (WTO), there is a shared "baseline" for their bilateral trade relations. For example, both nations grant the other nation "normal trade relations," or NTR, status as required under the WTO. Also, since Malaysia and the United States are both members of the Asia-Pacific Economic Cooperation (APEC), they are both committed to APEC's Bogor Goals of open trade and investment in Asia by 2020.[60] In addition, the United States and Malaysia concluded a trade and investment framework agreement (TIFA) in May 2004, are currently negotiating a free trade agreement (FTA), and are parties to various regional trade associations that are considering multilateral trade and investment agreements.

U.S.-Malaysia FTA

On March 8, 2006, the United States and Malaysia announced they would begin negotiating a bilateral free trade agreement (FTA).[61] The announcement was made by ex-U.S. Trade Representative Rob Portman and Malaysia's then-Minister of International Trade and Industry Rafidah Aziz on Capitol Hill with a bipartisan group of Members of Congress in attendance. The stated goals for the proposed FTA were to remove tariff and non-tariff trade barriers, and expand bilateral trade.

Since the announcement, The United States and Malaysia have held six rounds of negotiations concerning the terms of the proposed FTA.[62] The sixth round of talks were held in Kuala Lumpur on January 14-17, 2008.[63] Among the outstanding issues in the negotiations are: (1) market access for U.S. exports to Malaysia of agricultural goods, automobiles, and automotive parts and components; (2) market access for Malaysian exports to the United States of agricultural goods; (3) market access for U.S. services, especially financial services, in Malaysia; (4) Malaysia's enforcement of intellectual property rights (IPR) protection; and (5) Malaysia's government procurement system and its preferential treatment for businesses owned and operated by ethic Malays, or *bumiputera*.

Conditions for the fifth round of talks (held in Malaysia on February 5-8, 2007) were complicated at the end of January with the news of a $16 billion energy development deal between Malaysia's SKS Group and the National Iranian Oil Company that would develop Iranian gas fields and build liquefied natural gas plants.[64] Over the last six years, trade between Iran and Malaysia has grown rapidly. According to Malaysia's Department of Statistics, total trade between Malaysia and Iran rose from $224 million in 2000 to over $1.045 billion in 2007. In addition, Iran was Malaysia's third largest source of inward FDI in 2007 (see above).

During a House Committee on Foreign Affairs Hearing on January 31, 2007, then-Chairman Tom Lantos called the deal "abhorrent," and sent a letter to U.S. Trade Representative Susan Schwab requesting the suspension of negotiations on the proposed FTA until Malaysia renounced the deal with Iran.[65] U.S. Trade Representative Schwab indicated that she intended to continue the negotiations with Malaysia.[66]

Malaysia sharply rejected the call to revoke the energy deal with Iran. Aziz reportedly stated that the United States has no right to block Malaysia trading with any country, even after the conclusion of the proposed FTA.[67] Badawi also was firm on the issue, "We reject the pressure being inflicted upon us.... Do not bring any political matters into trade."[68] In an official statement on February 6, MITI repeated Malaysia's objections to Representative Lantos' comments, stating:

> The call by Tom Lantos to suspend the free trade agreement negotiations because of a business deal by a Malaysian company with the National Iranian Oil company does not augur well for the negotiations....

Malaysia reiterates that the FTA negotiations cannot be held hostage to any political demand, and cannot be conducted under such threats. Malaysia is also ready to suspend negotiations if the situation warrants it.[69]

Further complicating the negotiations was the passing of the April 2, 2007 deadline for consideration under Trade Promotion Authority.[70] Because President Bush did not notify Congress by the deadline, there are several scenarios under which Congress could consider the implementation bill for the proposed U.S.-Malaysia FTA.[71]

U.S.-Malaysia TIFA

On May 10, 2004, Malaysia and the United States signed a bilateral trade and investment framework agreement.[72] The U.S.-Malaysia TIFA states that both parties desire to develop trade and investment between the two countries, ensure that trade and environmental policies are supportive of sustainable development, and strengthen private sector contacts. To achieve these goals, the TIFA established a Joint Council on Trade and Investment, jointly chaired by Malaysia's Minister of International Trade and Industry and the U.S. Trade Representative, that is to meet at least once a year for the purpose of implementing the TIFA.

The U.S.-Malaysia TIFA also set out a two-part work program. The first part committed both nations to consultation on trade and investment liberalization and facilitation, with explicit consideration to trade in services, information and communications technology, biotechnology, and tourism. The second part stipulated that the United States and Malaysia will "examine the most effective means of reducing trade and investment barriers between them, including examination and consultations on the elements of a possible free trade agreement."

World Trade Organization (WTO)

Both the United States and Malaysia have been members of the World Trade Organization, or WTO, since its creation on January 1, 1995. While the United States is generally seen as being a consistent supporter of trade and investment liberalization, Malaysia's trade policy has undergone significant changes over the last 12 years. However, under the Bawadi Administration, Malaysia has generally been supportive of trade and investment liberalization.

For the current Doha Round, the United States and Malaysia are in general agreement on the overall goals of the talks, but have differed on some of the specifics. In particular, Malaysia joined its fellow ASEAN members in pushing the United States and the European Union to improve their market access offers for agricultural goods, including "making substantial reductions in trade distorting domestic support by the major players."[73]

Asia-Pacific Economic Cooperation (APEC)

The Asia-Pacific Economic Cooperation (APEC) group is another multilateral forum where the United States and Malaysia are both founding members. While Malaysia and the United States accept APEC's Bogor Goals for trade and investment liberalization by 2020, as well as APEC's "open regionalism" approach, there have been some differences of opinion on the future of APEC.[74] During the 2006 APEC meetings, The United States proposed the transformation of APEC into a Free Trade Area of the Asia-Pacific, or FTAAP. This proposal received a mixed response from other APEC members. Many observers believe that Malaysia prefers the formation of an all-Asian free trade area that would exclude the United States (see below).

Association of Southeast Asian Nations (ASEAN)

During its January 2007 summit in Cebu, ASEAN invited Australia, India, Japan, New Zealand, the People's Republic of China, and South Korea — the so-called "ASEAN+6" — to attend as part of the second East Asia Summit (EAS). The first EAS was held in Kulua Lumpur in December 2005.[75] ASEAN has also held talks about greater regional cooperation with just Japan, China, and South Korea — the ASEAN+3. ASEAN+3 met after ASEAN's last summit in Singapore in November 2007. Malaysia is a founding member of the Association of Southeast Asian Nations (ASEAN). ASEAN currently has 10 members; the United States is not a member.[76] East Timor has applied to become ASEAN member.

Malaysia is widely seen as a major supporter of the formation of an all-Asian free trade area that would exclude the United States. To some observers, Malaysia's support for the EAS is a continuation of Mahatir's East Asian

Economic Caucus and its predecessor, the East Asian Economic Group. According to one source, the goal of forming an all-Asian free trade area was endorsed after the second EAS by China after overcoming its reluctance to include Australia and India.[77] An attempt to forge a similar agreement during the 2005 East Asia Summit was unsuccessful.

The possible creation of an all-Asian free trade area is seen by some observers as a response to the growing influence of the European Union and the United States in international trade relations. For the United States, the proposed all-Asian free trade area is a rival model to its proposed FTAAP.

Malaysia is one of the five members of ASEAN that have ratified the new ASEAN Charter.[78] One of the main outcomes of the November summit in Singapore was the signing of a new charter on November 20, 2007. To be officially adopted, the new charter must be ratified by all 10 members of ASEAN. Even before the charter was signed, the Philippines indicated that it was unlikely to ratify the charter unless Burma (Myanmar) upheld the document's provisions on democracy and human rights.

Among its key provisions, the new charter commits the organization to its transformation into a regional economic community similar to the European Union by 2015. Included in its provisions are a collective commitment to the creation of an ASEAN Community "in which there is free flow of goods, services and investment; facilitated movement of business persons, professionals, talents and labour; and freer flow of capital." However, the charter also contains an "ASEAN minus X" provision that effectively allows any ASEAN member to opt out of economic commitments if it so chooses. It is unclear at this time how the creation of an ASEAN Community will affect U.S. policies in Southeast Asia.

OTHER ASPECTS OF U.S.-MALAYSIA RELATIONS

Bilateral relations between the United States and Malaysia are viewed as having improved since Badawi came to power. In the past, the relationship suffered from what a U.S. official called "blunt and intemperate public remarks"[79] critical of the United States by former Prime Minister Mahathir, who generally subscribed to a view of the United States as a neo-colonial power strongly under the influence of a coterie of Zionist Jews.[80] However, Mahathir's strong expression of sympathy and support following the attacks on September 11, 2001, apparently led to a thawing of a previously cool relationship that culminated with an official state visit to the White House by

Mahathir in May 2002.[81] The more cordial relationship between Malaysia and the United States has seemingly continued into the Badawi administration.

However, there are aspects of U.S.-Malaysia relations that periodically raise tensions between the two nations. In particular, Malaysia was and continues to be opposed to the U.S.-led invasion of Iraq, and frequently critiques the U.S. approach to counterterrorism as lacking balance. In addition, the United States has expressed misgivings about Malaysia's relationships with certain nations (in particular, Iran and Sudan) and continues to include Malaysia in the State Department's annual *Country Reports on Human Rights Practices*.

Prime Minister Badawi met with President Bush at the White House on July 19, 2004, during a three-day visit to the United States.[82] Badawi's visit sought to further strengthen the bilateral relationship between Malaysia and the United States following this important transfer of political leadership.[83] Malaysian Foreign Minister Syed Hamid Albar reportedly stated that Badawi would "exchange views on how we can deal with Islamic issues, how we can avoid the perception of prejudice, [and the] perception of marginalization of Muslims."[84] Badawi has also focused on strengthening already strong bilateral trade and investment ties between the United States and Malaysia.[85]

During his 2004 visit to Washington, Prime Minister Abdullah Badawi and President Bush reportedly discussed the need to move the bilateral relationship forward and rebuild confidence. Prime Minister Badawi reportedly told the president that "we need to find the moderate center, we must not be driven by extremist impulses or extremist elements ... we need to bridge the great divide that has been created between the Muslim world and the West."[86] During Badawi's visit, President Bush expressed his opinion that "the United States and Malaysia enjoy strong bilateral ties, ranging from trade and investment relationships to defense partnerships and active cooperation in the global war on terrorism. As a moderate Muslim nation, Malaysia offers the world an example of a modern, prosperous, multi-racial, and multi-religious society."[87]

U.S. Invasion of Iraq

Even before the invasion began, Malaysia was a vocal critic of a possible U.S.- led war against Saddam Hussain's government in Iraq. At an Extraordinary Islamic Summit Session of the OIC held in Doha on March 5, 2003 — two weeks before the war began — then-Prime Minister Mahathir stated Malaysia's opposition to war against Iraq.[88] In his speech to UMNO's 54th General Assembly on June 19, 2003, Mahathir said, "The hunt for the terrorists has made the world tense and unsafe. Bombs explode in many parts of the world. Afghanistan and Iraq were attacked and Syria and Iran were similarly threatened unless they changed their governments."[89]

Malaysia's opposition to the Iraq war and the continued U.S. presence in Iraq continued after Badawi became prime minister. In a speech at the Oxford Centre for Islamic Studies in January 2004, Badawi said, "The world must never forget that Iraq was illegally invaded. The world was told before the fact that the invasion was necessary because of an imminent threat posed by weapons of mass destruction. We know today that this reason was baseless."[90] During an UMNO party meeting in September 2004, Badawi reportedly said that Western countries had fueled international terrorism through the invasion of Iraq and their pro-Israel stance on the conflict between Israel and the Palestinians.[91] Later on that same month, in his speech before the United Nations General Assembly, Badawi stated, "Malaysia is convinced that the fight against terrorism cannot succeed through force of arms alone."[92] He went on to denounce "the increasing tendency to attribute linkages between international terrorism and Islam."[93] Badawi also indicated that he believed that the United Nations should be "given the lead role" in returning Iraq to a peaceful, stable nation.[94]

Although the rhetoric has changed in tone and tenor over the last four years, Malaysia opposition to the U.S. military presence in Iraq remains strong, and its disagreement with U.S. approach to terrorism continues. On January 15, 2008, Badawi stated:

> The fundamental point I am making is that religion in general, and the teachings of Islam in particular, cannot be faulted as either the reason for economic deprivation in the Muslim world or the source of the discord which persists between the Muslim world and the West. The problems which continue to fester in Afghanistan, Iraq, the Golan Heights, Lebanon and Palestine are vestiges of the projections of power by the centres of world power. The resulting humiliation being felt by Muslims is the real cause of their loss of trust and confidence towards the West.[95]

Counterterrorism

Though Malaysia opposed the U.S.-led invasion of Iraq, the United States considers Malaysia a valuable ally in the war against militant Islam in Southeast Asia. Southeast Asian Islamic populations in Brunei, Indonesia, and Malaysia (and to a lesser extent in Burma, the Philippines, Singapore, and Thailand) constitute a third of the world's Islamic population and are experiencing a spiritual, social, and cultural revival at a time when there is also increased radicalization among some groups in the region as demonstrated by the terrorist group Jemaah Islamiya (JI) and Abu Sayyaf.[96]

Malaysia reportedly estimated that there were 465 members of JI in Malaysia in 2003.[97] Malaysia has detained over 110 suspected terrorists since May 2001.[98] The Malaysian government believes that it has effectively crippled the Kumpulan Mujahedin Malaysia (KMM), which is thought to have had close ties with the Jemaah Islamiya (JI) terrorist group. The KMM sought the overthrow of the Malaysian government and the establishment of an Islamic state over Malaysia, Indonesia and Muslim parts of Southern Thailand and Southern Philippines. Two of JI's leaders, Noordin Mohammad Top and Azahari Husin, the later now captured, are Malaysian, though Top is thought to be a fugitive in Indonesia.[99]

The increasingly perceived comity of interests after September 11, 2001, improved the bilateral relationship. Foreign Minister Syed Hamid Albar stated in January of 2001 that Malaysia was looking forward to closer ties with the United States when President Bush assumed office.[100] The September 11, 2001 attacks against the United States were strongly criticized by former Prime Minister Mahathir, and the two nations subsequently began to work closely on counter-terror cooperation. Mahathir met with President Bush in Washington in May 2002, where they signed a memorandum of understanding on counterterrorism. Some Malaysian officials have, in general terms, equated the ISA with the USA Patriot Act. It has been argued that U.S. criticism of the ISA became muted following the passage of the USA Patriot Act.[101]

In May of 2002, the United States and Malaysia signed a declaration that provides a framework for counterterrorism cooperation.[102] Malaysia has taken a leading regional role in the war against terror by establishing a regional counterterrorism center in Kuala Lumpur that facilitates access to counterterror technology, information and training.[103] The concept for the center was announced in October 2002 following a meeting between President Bush and then-Deputy Prime Minister Badawi at the APEC meetings in

Mexico.[104] Malaysia hosted the ASEAN Regional Forum Inter-sessional Meeting on Counter-Terrorism in March of 2003.[105]

U.S. Coordinator for Counter-terrorism Ambassador Cofer Black emphasized the need to develop "sustained international political will and effective capacity building" to more effectively fight terrorism.[106] Within this context Ambassador Black made special reference to Malaysia's contribution to the war against terror in Asia. He identified Malaysia's opening of the Southeast Asia Regional Center for Counter-terrorism in August 2003 as a key example of counterterrorism capacity building in Asia. Other observers have questioned the degree to which the center has established its effectiveness. Since becoming Prime Minister, Badawi has continued Malaysia's commitment to fight terrorism.[107] While attending a regional counterterror conference in Bali, Indonesia in February 2004, then-U.S. Attorney General Ashcroft reportedly stated that the United States is very satisfied with the role that Malaysia has played in fighting terrorism and that Malaysia has provided a good example to countries in the region.[108]

However, during an address to a regional defense conference in Singapore in June 2004, Malaysian Defense Minister Najib Tun Razak admonished the West when he stated, "Let there be no doubt, there is more (terrorism) to come if we continue to ignore the need for a balanced approach to this campaign against terror.... We are concerned that powerful states may not be going about this campaign in ways that will win the hearts and minds of millions of ordinary people worldwide."[109] Some observers view this exchange as highlighting differences in regional Southeast Asian states' desires to include more "soft power" approaches to the war against terror as opposed to what they feel is an over reliance on "hard power" by the United States.

Military Cooperation

Military cooperation between the United States and Malaysia includes high-level defense visits, training exchanges, military equipment sales, expert exchanges and combined exercises. The 2007 Congressional Budget Justification for Foreign Operations states that "exposure to U.S. ideals promotes respect for human rights." It goes on to state that "the Malaysian military has not been involved in systemic violations of human rights."

In mid-2005, Deputy Secretary of State Zoellick and Malaysian Deputy Prime Minster Najib witnessed the renewal of an Acquisition and Cross Servicing Agreement that provides a framework for bilateral military cooperation.[110] Malaysian officers train in the United States under the International Military Education and Training (IMET) program and there is a student exchange program between the Malaysian Armed Forces Staff College and the U.S. Army Staff College at Fort Leavenworth. United States troops also travel to the Malaysian Army's Jungle Warfare Training Center in Pulada. Humanitarian assistance, disaster relief, anti-piracy, and counterterrorism are areas that have been identified as areas of mutual interest. Between 15 and 20 U.S. Navy ships visit Malaysia annually. Bilateral military exercises include all branches of the service.[111] Malaysia has also bought significant military equipment from the United States, including F-18/D aircraft. Recent military procurement is reportedly seeking to narrow the technology gap with small, but well armed, Singapore.[112] Such purchases will also likely help Malaysia secure its maritime interests in the Strait of Malacca and the South China Sea.

United States warships and U.S. military personnel go to Malaysia to participate in joint Cooperation Afloat Readiness and Training exercises with Malaysia in the South China Sea. The exercise is aimed at bolstering bilateral military ties and improving the ability of the United States Navy to operate in regional waters.[113] In an address in Malaysia in June 2004, Admiral Fargo pointed to shared concerns over "transnational problems," including "terrorism and proliferation, trafficking in humans and drugs and piracy" and emphasized that "we have tremendous respect for sovereignty."[114] The United States has sent Coast Guard officers to the Marine Patrol training Center in Johor Baharu to help train Malaysian officers in maritime enforcement. Malaysia established a Maritime Enforcement Agency in 2005 to increase maritime patrols.[115] Over 50,000 ships a year pass through the Straits of Malacca. Some ships have been vulnerable to piracy in the 600 mile long strait. There is also concern that terrorists could seek to mount an attack against shipping in the strategically vital strait.[116]

After some apparent mis-communication, Malaysia and the United States reportedly have come to a mutual understanding on how best to secure the Straits of Malacca, which are territorial waters from possible terrorist acts.[117] An estimated 30% of world trade and half of the world's oil transits through the Straits of Malacca.[118] Testifying before the House Armed Services Committee on March 31, 2004, Admiral Thomas Fargo, Commander of the U.S. Pacific Command, identified the Straits of Malacca off Malaysia's coast as an area where there is concern that international terrorists might seek to attack shipping or seize a ship to use as a weapon. Fargo also reportedly suggested the idea that U.S. counterterrorism forces be positioned in the area to be able to deal with such a threat. This idea reportedly was announced without prior consultation with Malaysia, which reportedly responded "coolly" to the suggestion.[119] Malaysia reportedly prefers an arrangement, in the words of Defense Minister Najib, where "the actual interdiction will be done by the littoral states."[120] This approach was subsequently supported by Fargo during a visit to Malaysia, where he reportedly stated that U.S. cooperation would focus on intelligence sharing and capacity building to assist regional states in addressing the potential threat.[121] On July 20, 2004, Malaysia, Indonesia, and Singapore began coordinated naval patrols of the Straits of Malacca.[122]

Human Rights

The State Department report on human rights practices in Malaysia stated that the Malaysian government "generally respected the human rights of its citizens; however, there were problems in some areas."[123] Among the problems remaining are: abridgement of citizens' right to change their government, detentions of persons without trial, restrictions on freedom of the press, restrictions on freedom of assembly and association, ethnic discrimination, and incomplete investigation of detainee deaths. The report also mentioned that "the civilian authorities generally maintained effective control of the security forces."[124]

Relations with Sudan

Although official bilateral trade in 2007 was small (less than $53 million in exports and only $42 million in imports), Prime Minister Badawi has publically stated that Malaysia hopes to increase trade and investment relations with Sudan. Malaysia already plays an important role in Sudan's trade with other nations. Malaysian companies — along with companies from China, France, India, Kuwait, and the United Kingdom — are reportedly major investors in Sudan's petroleum industry. In 2005, the Sudanese government received $2.3 billion in revenues from petroleum exports.[125] The Malaysian newspaper, *The New Straits Times*, reports that Malaysia is the second largest investor in Sudan, after China.[126] Malaysian companies reportedly provide substantial construction and transportation services to Sudan's oil industry. Petronas, Malaysia's state oil company, has interests in nine oil fields in Sudan, plus a refinery project on Port Sudan.[127]

Malaysia is the current chair of the Organization of the Islamic Conference (OIC); Sudan is also a member. During an April 2007 trip to Sudan, Prime Minister Badawi expressed some support for its fellow OIC member, saying the situation in Darfur was being exaggerated by the media.[128] In addition, Malaysia would "approach the leaders of the Organization of the Islamic Conference and Islamic Development Bank to extend whatever help that can be given to the government of Sudan."[129]

Malaysia also opposes proposed U.N. sanctions on Sudan. In the opinion of Prime Minister Badawi, the sanctions would hurt the people of Malaysia.[130] Instead, Malaysia prefers to allow more time for talks between the United Nations and Sudan. The United States has so far held off on unilateral sanctions on Sudan to give the United Nations time to convince Sudan to permit U.N. peacekeepers into Darfur. However, during Prime Minister Badawi's visit to Sudan, Sudan's President Omer Hassan Ahmed Al-Bashir told reporters he hoped Malaysia would help Sudan "confront Western pressure to accept international forces in Darfur."[131]

U.S. Assistance

U.S. assistance to Malaysia is relatively modest in size, and has been declining in value over the last four years. United States foreign assistance to Malaysia has included International Military Education and Training (IMET), Non-Proliferation Anti-Terrorist Demining and Related Programs (NADR), Anti-Terrorism Assistance (ATA), and Export Control and Related Border Security Assistance (EXBS). For FY2009, the Bush Administration has requested funding for International Narcotics Control and Law Enforcement.

Figure 1. Map of Malaysia.

IMET programs with Malaysia seek to contribute to regional stability by strengthening military-to-military ties and familiarizing the Malaysian military with U.S. military doctrine, equipment, and management that promotes interoperability. The U.S. is a leading training partner with Malaysia at its Southeast Asia Regional Counter-terrorism Center.

**Table 8. Bilateral Assistance
(in millions of dollars)**

Account	FY2007 actual	FY2008 estimate	FY2009 request
International Military Education and Training (IMET)	0.871	0.876	0.750
International Narcotics Control and Law Enforcement	-	-	0.400
Non-Proliferation Anti-Terrorist Demining and Related Programs (NADR)	2.401	1.998	1.540
Totals	3.272	2.874	2.690

Source: State Department, FY 2007 Congressional Budget Justification for Foreign Operations, Released March 11, 2008. See also CRS Report RL31362, U.S. Foreign Aid to East and South Asia: Selected Recipients, by Thomas Lum.

End Notes

[1] At that time, UMNO was part of a political coalition known as the Alliance Party, a predecessor to the BN.
[2] Malaysia has a bicameral parliament consisting of the elected *Dewan Rakyat*, the lower house, and the largely-appointed *Dewan Negara* (National Hall), the upper house.
[3] Under Malaysian law, a parliamentary election must be held at least every five years. However, in many cases, early elections were held after about four years.
[4] "Nik Aziz Likens Big Win to a Tsunami," *The Star*, March 9, 2008.
[5] The State of Sarawak did not hold concurrent elections.
[6] Jane Ritikos, "Examine Losses, Says Dr. M," *The Star*, March 10, 2008.
[7] "Abdullah Announces Cabinet Line-Up, Half of Administration New Faces," *Bernama*, March 18, 2008.
[8] "Samy: Time Not Ripe for Barisan to be a Single Party," *The Star*, March 17, 2008.
[9] Ibid.
[10] Claudia Theophilus, "Malaysia PM: Lessons to be Learnt," *Al Jazeera*, March 11, 2008. Malays and other indigenous groups are known as *bumiputeras*, or "sons of the soil."

[11] Barbara Watson Andaya and Leonard Y. Andaya, *A Brief History of Malaysia*, University of Hawaii Press, 2001; Harold Crouch, *Government and Society in Malaysia*, Cornell University Press, 1996.

[12] Lt. General David Patraeus has reportedly studied the Malaya Emergency, among other counterinsurgency operations, as he has prepared himself for operations in Iraq. Dan Murphy, "New Commander, New Plan in Iraq," *Christian Science Monitor*, February 9, 2007.

[13] Stuart Drummond and David Hawkins, "The Malaysian Elections of 1969: An Analysis of the Campaign and the Results," *Asian Survey*, Vol. 10, No. 4 (April 1970), pp. 320-335.

[14] YAB Dato' Seri Dr. Mahathir Mohamad, *Vision 2020*, (Kuala Lumpur: Institute of Strategic and International Studies, 1991).

[15] Crouch, pp. 4-5.

[16] William Case, "Malaysia's General Elections in 1999: A Consolidated and High-Quality Semi-Democracy," *Asian Studies Review*, March, 2001.

[17] Crouch, p. 5.

[18] For a more detailed discussion of these dynamics see William Case, "Deep Insecurity and Political Stability: Inside Mahathir's Malaysia," in Bruce Vaughn ed. *The Unraveling of Island Asia?* (Westport: Praeger Publishers, 2002).

[19] S. Jayasankaran, "Lost Ground," *Far Eastern Economic Review*, March 21, 2002.

[20] "Malaysia's Election: Bravo Badawi," *The Economist*, March 27, 2004.

[21] See Anthony Smith, "Malaysia's 2004 Elections: Mahathir's Successor Succeeds," *Asia Pacific Security Studies*, April 5, 2004 and "So Much for the New Broom," *The Economist*, April 3, 2004.

[22] The term "Islamist" is used to identify those who would affiliate themselves with more extreme interpretations of Islam.

[23] "Abdullah Pledges to Work Hard to Make Vision 2020 a Reality," *New Straits Times*, September 8, 2003.

[24] Bridget Welsh, "Elite Contestation, Political Dilemmas and Incremental Change," Woodrow Wilson Center, July 24, 2003.

[25] Badawi's father and grandfather were Islamic religious scholars. Badawi himself has a degree in Islamic Studies.

[26] "Malaysia: Country Report," *The Economist Intelligence Unit*, February 2007.

[27] Transcript of Interview with the Prime Minister of Malaysia," *Bernama*, February 17, 2005.

[28] "Malaysian Premier calls on Muslims to Defy Militants," *Agence France Presse*, July 20, 2005.

[29] Paul Wiseman, "In Malaysia Islamic Civilization is Promoted," *USA Today*, November 4, 2004. Evelyn Goh, "Keeping Southeast Asia on the U.S. Radar Screen," *PacNet Newsletter*, May 26, 2005.

[30] Mohamad Nawab Mohd Osman, "Where to Islam Hadhari?" *IDSS Commentaries*, November 28, 2006.

[31] "The United States and Malaysia: A Diverse and Expanding Partnership," U.S. Department of State, Bureau of Public Affairs, July 26, 2006.

[32] S. Jayasankaran, "Well-Oiled," *Far Eastern Economic Review*, August 28, 2003.

[33] S. Jayasankaran, "Oil and Water," *Far Eastern Economic Review*, July 3, 2003.

[34] For additional information see CRS Report RL33242, *East Asia Summit (EAS): Issues for Congress*, by Bruce Vaughn.

[35] Singapore was the first member to ratify the new charter on December 18, 2007. Since then, Brunei, Laos, Malaysia, and Vietnam have ratified the charter. Burma (Myanmar), Cambodia, Indonesia, the Philippines, and Thailand have not ratified the new charter.

[36] Jane Perlez, "Asian Leaders Find China a More Cordial Neighbor," *The New York Times*, 18 October, 2003.

[37] Alice D. Ba, "China and ASEAN: Re-navigating Relations for a 21st Century Asia," *Asia Survey,* August, 2003.

[38] Rommel Banlaoi, "Southeast Asian Perspectives on the Rise of China: Regional Security After 9/11." *Parameters,* Summer, 2003.

[39] J. Wong and S. Chan, "China-ASEAN Free Trade Agreement," *Asian Survey*, June, 2003.

[40] Vijay Joshi, "Ethnic Tensions in Malaysian Election," *Associated Press*, March 6, 2008.

[41] "Crackdown on Undocumented Workers Ends ... for Now," *Asia News*, February 2, 2005.

[42] For more information on human trafficking between Indonesia and Malaysia, see the U.S. State Department's *Trafficking in Persons Report*, June 2007.

[43] "Malaysia at a Glance: 2005-06," Economist Intelligence Unit, June 2005.

[44] "M'sia to Send Peace Monitors to Aceh," *Bernama Daily,* August 6, 2005.

[45] "Malaysia Says Southeast Asian Grouping Should Tackle Defence Issues," *Agence France Presse,* August 7, 2005.

[46] "Indonesian Fires Blanket Central Malaysia," *The New York Times,* August 12, 2005.

[47] "Malaysia Must Prosecute Cos for Haze-Indonesia," *Dow Jones,* August 14, 2005, and "Govt Vows to Prosecute 10 Firms Over Forest Fires," *The Jakarta Post,* August 16, 2005.

[48] "Malaysia: Pollution Levels Close Schools," *Asia Pacific Radio,* August 11, 2005.

[49] Jared Diamond, *Collapse: How Societies Choose to Fail of Succeed* (New York: Viking Publishers, 2005), p. 471.

[50] "Malaysia, Thailand Prepare to Accelerate Development of Border Regions," BBC News, February 12, 2007. "Malaysia Pledges to Aid Thai Government in Ending Violent Unrest on Shared Border," Global Insight, February 12, 2007.

[51] For an overview of Malaysia-Singapore relations, see K.S. Nathan, "Malaysia-Singapore Relations: Retrospect and Prospect," *Contemporary Southeast Asia*, vol. 24, no. 2 (August 2002), pp. 385-410.

[52] "Bilateral Ties Not Affected," *New Strait Times*, March 25, 2008.

[53] The 1998 recession was precipitated by the Asian Financial Crisis (see CRS Report RL30517, *Asian Financial Crisis and Recovery: Status and Implications for U.S. Interests* by Richard Cronin for details). The 2001 downturn is generally attributed to the global economic downturn following the attacks on the Pentagon and World Trade Center (see CRS Report RS21937, *9/11 Terrorism: Global Economic Costs*, by Dick Nanto for details).

[54] "Bank Negara Lowers 2008 Growth Target," *New Strait Times*, March 26, 2008.

[55] For a list of the World Bank's ranking of economies by per capita income, see [http://siteresources.worldbank.org/DATASTATISTICS/Resources/GNIPC.pdf].

[56] For more details about the Ninth Malaysia Plan, see its webpage, [http://www.epu.jpm.my/rm9/html/overview.htm].

[57] Following the Asian Financial Crisis of 1997, the value of the ringgit fell from 2.5 ringgits to US$1, to over 4 ringgits to the US$1. In September 1998, the Bank Negara Malaysia pegged the exchange rate at 3.5 ringgits to US$1.

[58] With the exception of the spring of 2007, the value of the ringgit has stayed within 2% of the value of the renminbi since China adopted a crawling peg in July 2005.

[59] Source of FDI data: Malaysian Industrial Development Authority, or MIDA [http://www.mida.gov.my/].

[60] For more information about APEC and its Bogor Goals, see CRS Report RL31038, *Asia Pacific Economic Cooperation (APEC) and the 2007 Meetings in Sydney, Australia*, by Michael F. Martin.
[61] "United States, Malaysia Announce Intention to Negotiate Free Trade Agreement," U.S. Trade Representative's website: [http://www.ustr.gov/Document_Library/Press_Releases/ 2006/March/United_States,_Malaysia_Announce_Intention_to_Negotiate_Free_Trade_ Agreement.html].
[62] For details about the proposed FTA and its negotiation, see CRS Report RL33445, *The Proposed U.S.-Malaysia Free Trade Agreement*, by Michael F. Martin.
[63] An informal round of talks were held in Washington, DC on April 13, 2007.
[64] "Malaysia Stands by Iranian Gas Deal," *BBC News*, February 2, 2007.
[65] "Remarks by Congressman Tom Lantos, Chairman, House Committee on Foreign Affairs, at Hearing, 'Understanding the Iran Crisis,'" January 31, 2007.
[66] Reported in *Washington Trade Daily*, February 5, 2007.
[67] "Malaysia Defends State Despite U.S. Threat to Halt FTA Talks," *Bernama – Malaysian National News Agency*, February 2, 2007.
[68] "Malaysia Stands by Iranian Gas Deal," *BBC News*, February 2, 2007.
[69] "Statement by the Ministry of International Trade and Industry on US Congressman Tom Lantos Request to Suspend Malaysia-US FTA Negotiations," February 6, 2007.
[70] For a more detailed discussion of Trade Promotion Authority, see CRS Report RL33743, "Trade Promotion Authority (TPA): Issues, Options, and Prospects for Renewal," by J. F. Hornbeck and William H. Cooper.
[71] For a discussion of those scenarios, see CRS Report RL33445, *The Proposed U.S.-Malaysia Free Trade Agreement*, by Michael F. Martin.
[72] The full text of the TIFA is available at the U.S. Trade Representative's website at [http://www.ustr.gov/assets
[73] "Statement on the Doha Development Agenda of the WTO," January 13, 2007.
[74] For more information on APEC, see CRS Report RL31038, *Asia Pacific Economic Cooperation (APEC) and the 2006 Meetings in Hanoi, Vietnam*, by Michael F. Martin.
[75] For more information about the first EAS Summit, see CRS Report RL33242, *East Asia Summit (EAS): Issues for Congress*, by Bruce Vaughn.
[76] The current ASEAN members are: Brunei Darussalam, Cambodia, Indonesia, Laos, Malaysia, Myanmar (Burma), Philippines, Singapore, Thailand, and Vietnam.
[77] "Asian Leaders Plan Free-Trade Area from India to New Zealand," by Arijit Ghosh and Francisco Alcuaz, Jr. *Bloomberg*, January 15, 2007.
[78] The other four members to have ratified the new charter are Brunei, Laos, Singapore, and Vietnam.
[79] Prepared Statement of Matthew Daley, Deputy Assistant Secretary, Bureau of East Asian and Pacific Affairs, U.S. Department of State, As submitted to the Committee on International Relations House of Representatives, Subcommittee on Asia and the Pacific, March 26, 2003.
[80] Alan Sipress, "Malaysia Calls on Muslims to resist Jewish Influence," *Washington Post*, October 17, 2003.
[81] Pamela Sodhy, "U.S.-Malaysian Relations during the Bush Administration: The Political, Economic, and Security Aspects," *Contemporary Southeast Asia*, vol. 25, no. 3 (2003), pp. 363-86.
[82] The two heads of state have met on other occasions, but the 2004 visit has been the only official state visit to the White House.

[83] Malaysian Prime Minister to Meet with U.S. President 19 July," *BBC Monitoring Asia Pacific*, July 6, 2004.

[84] "Malaysian Leader to Tell Bush Terrorism Has Increased," *Associated Press*, July 9, 2004.

[85] "Abdullah's Leadership Style Gets Positive Response From Leaders," *Bernama Daily*, July 9, 2004.

[86] Speech by The Honourable Abdullah Ahmad Badawi, Prime Minister of Malaysia, Dinner Hosted by the U.S.- ASEAN Business Council, Washington, DC July 19, 2004.

[87] President Bush, *Written Remarks to the U.S. ASEAN Business Council Dinner Honoring Prime Minister Badawi*, July 19, 2004.

[88] Speech by Prime Minister Mahathir, Extraordinary Islamic Summit Session of the OIC, March 5, 2003.

[89] Speech by Prime Minister Mahathir, 54th UMNO National Assembly, June 19, 2003.

[90] Speech by Prime Minister Badawi, Oxford Centre for Islamic Studies, January 20, 2004.

[91] "Malaysia Accuses West of Fueling Terrorism," AFP, September 23, 2004.

[92] Address of Prime Minister Badawi, United Nations General Assembly, September 27, 2004.

[93] Ibid.

[94] Ibid.

[95] Statement by the Honourable Abdullah Ahmad Badawi Prime Minister of Malaysia on the Occasion of the First Alliance of Civilizations Annual Forum, January 15, 2008.

[96] S. MacDonald and J. Lemco, "Political Islam in Southeast Asia," *Current History*, November, 2002. For additional information, see CRS Report RL31672, *Terrorism in Southeast Asia*, coordinated by Bruce Vaughn.

[97] Bridget Welsh, "Malaysia: Security Begins at Home," in David Wiencek and William Carpenter, *Asian Security Handbook: Terrorism and the New Security Environment*, (Armonk: M.E. Sharpe, 2005).

[98] Country Reports on Terrorism, 2005, United States Department of State, Released April 2006 and J. Chao, "Malaysia's War on Terror Worries Rights Advocates," *American Statesman*, November 10, 2002.

[99] Country Reports on Terrorism, 2005, United States Department of State, Released April 2006.

[100] "Looking Forward to Warmer Ties in Post-Clinton Era," *New Straits Times*, January 10, 2001.

[101] Sodhy, op. cit.

[102] "Malaysia, USA Sign Anti-terror Declaration," *BBC Monitoring Service*, May 15, 2002.

[103] R. Hamsawi, "Local Funding for Anti-Terror Center," *New Straits Times*, April 3, 2003.

[104] "Malaysia: Minister Gives Details of ASEAN Anti-terror Centre Project," *BBC Monitoring Service*, April 2, 2003.

[105] See CRS Report RL31672, "Terrorism in Southeast Asia" for further information on terrorism in Southeast Asia.

[106] United States Department of State, *Patterns of Global Terrorism, 2003*, April, 2004.

[107] "Malaysia Pledges Terror Fight," *The Wall Street Journal*, November 4, 2003.

[108] "U.S. Compliments Malaysia for Role in Anti-terrorism Efforts," *Bernama Daily*, February 5, 2004.

[109] "Malaysia Says U.S. Needs to be More Balanced in Its War Against Terrorism," *International Customwire*, June 6, 2004.

[110] "Malaysia's Efforts Against Terror," *Bernama*, June 8, 2005.

[111] Huhtala, April 14, 2003.

[112] S. Jayasankaran, "Malaysia: Call for Arms," *Far Eastern Economic Review*, May 16, 2003.

[113] "U.S. Navy Task Force to Head for RP," *Manila Times*, July 14, 2004.

[114] Admiral Thomas Fargo, Commander, U.S. Pacific Command, Malaysia Media Roundtable, June 23, 2004.
[115] "24 Hour Surveillance for the Malacca Strait," *Bernama*, March 11, 2005.
[116] "Malaysia to Beef Up Malacca Patrols,"*Agence France Presse*, February 6, 2007.
[117] For a discussion of threats to shipping in the strait and regional responses see Bronson Percival, *Indonesia and the United States: Shared Interest in Maritime Security*, U.S.-Indonesia Society, June 2005.
[118] "Malaysia Accepts U.S. Aid, But Not Patrol, In Strait," *International Herald Tribune*, June 22, 2004 and Prime Minister of Singapore Lee Hsien Loong,"Engaging a New Asia," Washington, July 12, 2005.
[119] "Indonesia, Malaysia Give Cool Response to Suggestion of U.S. Troops in Malacca Strait," *Voice of America Press Release*, April 7, 2004.
[120] "Malaysia, United States to Discuss Security in the Straits of Malacca," *International Custom Wire*, June 6, 2004.
[121] See "U.S. to Render Assistance to Littoral States of Malacca Strait," *International Customwire*, June 23, 2004 and "U.S. Navy Task Force to Head for RP," *Manila Times*, July 14, 2004.
[122] "Indonesia: Three Nations Patrol Straits," *Stratfor*, July 20, 2004.
[123] U.S. Department of State, *Country Reports on Human Rights Practices - 2007*.
[124] Ibid.
[125] "Divestment Campaign Targeting Sudan over Darfur Goes Global," *Associated Press*, May 1, 2007.
[126] "Malay sia to Help Sudan with More Investments," *The New Straits Times*, April 17, 2007.
[127] "Malaysia PM Visits Darfur, Seeks Firmer Sudan Ties," *Reuters*, April 18, 2007.
[128] "No Sanctions on Sudan: Malaysia," *Bernama*, April 17, 2007.
[129] "Malaysia PM Visits Darfur, Seeks Firmer Sudan Ties," *Reuters*, April 18, 2007.
[130] "No Sanctions on Sudan: Malaysia," *Bernama*, April 17, 2007.
[131] "Malaysia to Help Sudan with More Investments," *The New Straits Times*, April 17, 2007.

In: Malaysia: Country Profile and U.S. Relations ISBN: 978-1-61470-172-9
Editors: G. A. Villalobos, D. E. Segura © 2011 Nova Science Publishers, Inc.

Chapter 3

THE PROPOSED U.S.-MALAYSIA FREE TRADE AGREEMENT[*]

Michael F. Martin

SUMMARY

This report addresses the proposed U.S.-Malaysia free trade agreement (FTA). It provides an overview of the current status of the negotiations, a review of the 2008 talks, an examination of leading issues that have arisen during the negotiations, a review of U.S. interests in the proposed agreement, a summary of the potential effects of a FTA on bilateral trade, and an overview of the legislative procedures to be followed if the proposed FTA is presented to Congress for approval.

The proposed U.S.-Malaysia FTA is of interest to Congress because (1) it requires congressional approval; (2) it would continue the past trend toward greater trade liberalization and globalization; (3) it may include controversial provisions; and (4) it could affect trade flows for certain sensitive goods and industries in the United States.

Since the U.S. Trade Representative announced on March 8, 2006, the Bush Administration's intent to negotiate a free trade agreement with Malaysia, eight rounds of negotiations have been held. A proposed ninth round of talks scheduled for November 2008 were postponed until after President Barack Obama's inauguration once it became apparent that

---

[*] This is an edited, reformatted and augmented version of a Congressional Research Service publication, CRS Report for Congress RL 33445, from www.crs.gov, dated January 26, 2009.

several outstanding issues remained unresolved. Since the postponement, Malaysia has suspended the bilateral negotiations, possibly in response to U.S. support for Israel's military operations in Gaza.

Efforts in 2008 to complete the FTA negotiations by the end of the Bush Administation were unsuccessful. There is general agreement that one major "sticking point" is Malaysia's government procurement policies, which give preferential treatment for certain types of Malaysian-owned companies. Other key outstanding provisions of the possible FTA as of the end of 2008 were intellectual property rights protection, protection of Malaysia's agricultural and automotive industry, and trade in services.

Areas of particular interest to U.S. exporters include a reduction of Malaysian trade barriers to automobiles and certain agricultural products, provisions for the enforcement of intellectual property rights, and broader access to Malaysia's service sectors such as financial services, telecommunications, and professional services.

Both nations could potentially see economic benefits from the proposed FTA, but there will be both winners and losers in both nations, as well as in other nations not part of the bilateral agreement. Overall bilateral trade flows would probably rise, possibly at the expense of some domestic and foreign manufacturers and their workers. In 2007, the United States was Malaysia's largest trading partner, while Malaysia was the United States' tenth largest trading partner. The United States was Malaysia's top export market and its second largest supplier of imports in 2007.

In addition, the United States may also accrue some political benefits from the proposed FTA. An FTA with Malaysia would strengthen U.S. ties with a moderate, democratic Muslim nation. It would also support U.S. efforts to be viewed as more engaged in Southeast Asia.

OVERVIEW OF THE CURRENT STATUS OF NEGOTIATIONS

On March 8, 2006, then U.S. Trade Representative (USTR) Rob Portman announced and notified Congress of the Administration's intent to negotiate a free trade agreement (FTA) with Malaysia..[1] At the time, then USTR Portman indicated that he thought the negotiations could be completed "within a year."[2]

The first round of negotiations was held June 12-16, 2006, in Malaysia with at least five rounds anticipated. Since then, eight separate rounds of talks have been held. A proposed ninth round of talks were postponed until after President Barack Obama's inauguration. If and when the negotiations are completed, the proposed FTA will have to be submitted to Congress for consideration if it is to go into effect.[3]

Conserted efforts to complete the negotiations of the free trade agreement (FTA) before the end of the Bush Administration were unsuccessful as talks foundered on a number of key issues. These include Malaysia's government procurement policies (which give preferential treatment to *bumiputera*-owned companies),[4] market access for U.S. companies into Malaysia's services sectors (in particular, financial services), provisions for intellectual property rights (IPR) protection, and market access for U.S. exports of automobiles and agricultural crops. During a media roundtable discussion in December 2008, U.S. Ambassador to Malaysia James Keith indicated that there were 23 trading issues still to be resolved in the negotiations.[5]

The FTA negotiations continued to be a controversial topic in Malaysia in 2008. An ad-hoc meeting of senior government officials reconfirmed its support for continuing FTA negotiations on certain topics, including government procurement, competition policy, intellectual property rights, and labor conditions.[6] However, some issues – such as rice imports – remained off the table. In addition, the financial crisis in the United States apparently raised some concerns in Malaysia about discussions over opening up Malaysia's financial markets to U.S. companies. Also, various interest groups in Malaysia – including an organization representing Malaysia's small and medium-sized enterprises (SMEs) – reiterated their call for the Malaysian government to terminate the FTA negotiations, claiming that the proposed agreement would do irreparable harm to thousands of Malaysia's SMEs.[7] In November 2008, Tony Pua of Parti Tindakan Demokratik (Democratic Action Party, or DAP), a major opposition party, suggested the government prepare a "white paper" outlining the details of the FTA negotiations to be presented to Malaysia's parliament to assure that the negotiation team was abiding by the agreed government policies.[8]

The future status of the proposed FTA were further complicated by Israel's military operation in Gaza.[9] After Israel launched "Operation Cast Lead" on December 27, 2008, various political figures and interest groups in Malaysia called for a boycott of U.S. products and the suspension of the FTA talks to protest U.S. support for Israel's military operations in Gaza. On January 12, 2009, Malaysia's Minister of International Trade and Industry, Muhyiddin Yassin, said that FTA talks with the United States were temporarily being stopped until the ministry received further instructions from Malaysia's Cabinet.[10] Minister Muhyiddin[11] added that Malaysia would not be hasty to conclude the FTA negotiations at a time when the United States was supporting "Israel's cruelty to Palestinian people."[12]

There have been some indications from the Obama Administration about its intentions regarding the U.S.-Malaysia FTA negotiations. Following the U.S. presidential elections, Minister Muhyiddin stated that the Malaysian government had been informed by representatives of the incoming Obama Administration that negotiations would recommence sometime after the inauguration.[13] There have also been signals from President Obama that workers rights and environmental issues will play a more prominent role in trade negotiations during his Administration. In his announcement to nominate Ron Kirk as U.S. Trade Representative, then President-Elect Obama stated, "As a leader, negotiator, and principled proponent of trade, Ron will help make sure that any agreements I sign as President protect the rights of all workers, promote the interests of all Americans, and preserve the planet we all share."[14]

REVIEW OF 2008 NEGOTIATIONS

At one time, there were to be three rounds of talks in 2008, to be held in January, July and November, respectively. In the end, only two rounds of talks were held (in January and July as planned), but the third round of talks were postponed at the request of the United States.

Following the failure to complete FTA negotiations in 2007, there was a perception in Malaysia that the Bush Administration did not see relations with Malaysia or the conclusion of FTA negotiations as a priority. During a press interview in December 2007, Ambassador Keith was asked if the failure of U.S. Secretary of State Condoleezza Rice to attend ASEAN meetings, as well as the "low-level delegation" sent by the United States to Malaysia's 50th National Day celebrations, was an indication that Malaysia had "moved down the list of priorities for the U.S. State Department."[15] Ambassador Keith reassured the press of the U.S. commitment to the region and to Malaysia, pointing to the passage on September 17, 2007 of House Resolution 518 commemorating Malaysia's 50th anniversary as evidence.

On December 30, 2007, U.S. Assistant Trade Representative Barbara Weisel confirmed that "the U.S. continues to seek to conclude the agreement by this summer, which we believe is achievable..."[16] Weisel also said that the Bush Administration would seek an "appropriate vehicle" to obtain congressional approval of the proposed FTA once the negotiations were completed.[17]

The Seventh Round of Talks

On January 14, 2008, Malaysia and the United States began their seventh round of formal negotiations in Kuala Lumpur over the terms of a possible U.S.-Malaysia Free Trade Agreement. In a statement to the press on the day the talks began, U.S. embassy spokeswoman Kathryn Taylor said the United States was seeking "real, demonstrable progress" during the seventh round of talks, but also pointed out that "there is no deadline" for completing the agreement.[18] However, in an interview with the press that same day, Ambassador Keith stated he was hoping that the negotiations would be completed by the middle of 2008.[19]

Assessments of the outcome of the seventh round of talks were mixed. A news story from China reported that four key issues were discussed during the talks—investment, trade in goods and services, intellectual property rights, and "legal issues."[20] According to *Xinhua*, the United States was "hopeful of concluding its free trade agreement with Malaysia by this summer ... "[21]

Malaysia's official news agency, *Bernama*, provided a similar positive assessment of the seventh round of talks, quoting Assistant USTR Weisel, "We have largely reached the goal set for the week. The two sides have moved significantly on a wide range of issues ... progress we made this week is encouraging."[22] The *New Straits Times* of Malaysia published a similar story on the talks on January 18, 2008, referring to the progress that had been made and possibility of concluding the negotiations by summer.[23]

Press accounts of the status of the FTA talks turned less optimistic a few days later. On January 24, 2008, *Bernama* printed two separate stories on the FTA negotiations. The first article reported that then Minister of International Trade and Industry Rafidah Abdul Aziz saw no need for a deadline for concluding the trade talks.[24] The second article stated that Ambassador Keith had indicated that if the FTA with Malaysia were not completed by the end of July, the United States would focus its attention on other FTA agreements.[25] Ambassador Keith was quoted as saying, "We will turn our attention to seal the pacts with South Korea and Columbia before the end of the Bush Administration. There will be no hard feelings."[26]

Another negative sign about the status of the negotiations was the lack of a decision on the date and place to hold the next round of talks. The United States stated that there was agreement on "the next steps"—communicating on a full set of issues still to be resolved and setting the dates for the next round of talks.[27] However, Minister Rafidah reportedly said on the status of the negotiations, "Whatever issues that can be cleared first, they have cleared. We don't have to meet again."[28]

The Eighth Round of Talks

The eighth round of negotiations were held in Washington, DC on July 14 – 18, 2008. Heading the Malaysian delegation was the Secretary General of the Minister of International Trade and Industry (MITI), Abdul Rahman Mamat. The chief negotiator for the U.S. government was Assistant USTR Weisel. The negotiations focused on the topics of six working groups addressing trade in agricultural goods, trade in services, investment, IPR, sanitary and phytosanitary (SPS) measures, and legal provisions.

Political events in both nations overshadowed the negotiations. The upcoming U.S. presidential elections and the resulting change in administration influenced the talks, as did the the poor showing of the ruling Barisan Nasional (BN) in Malaysia's general elections of March 8, 2008.[29] In addition, the uncertain status of the proposed U.S. FTAs with Colombia and South Korea may have had an impact on the talks. While the Bush Administration has expressed a desire to conclude the negotiations prior to the end of its term, the Malaysian government had indicated that it saw no need to rush to conclude the talks in 2008.

For the United States, the key issue for the July 2008 talks was greater foreign access to Malaysian government procurement contracts. According to Malaysia, while the topics of competition policy, environment, labor, and financial services could be discussed, any agreement reached on these topics would be non-binding.[30] Other areas under discussion were market access for U.S. agricultural exports and service providers. Prior to the meetings, the newly-appointed Minister of International Trade and Industry, Muhyiddin Yassin, stated that Malaysia would not compromise in "several sensitive areas, such as agriculture."[31] Malaysia has specifically excluded rice from consideration in the FTA negotiations.

There were indications of some progress during the eighth round of negotiations. In a press statement following the talks, MITI indicated that the two nations were "exploring possibilities of business collaboration and capacity-building in the services sector within the framework of the Malaysia-U.S. FTA."[32] Assistant USTR Weisel said that the United States hoped that Malaysia's proposed reforms of its government procurement process may help advance FTA negotiations on the issue.[33] U.S. hopes received some encouragement in October 2008, when Minister Muhyiddin announced that Malaysia's Cabinet had indicated its willingness to move government procurement from the list of "no talk" issues to one where non-binding discussions would be allowed.[34]

The Malaysian Institute of Economic Research (MIER) observed after the July 2008 negotiations that the United States had adopted a "pragmatic approach," possibly due to its problems with its proposed FTAs with South Korea and Thailand. MIER Executive Director Mohamed Ariff Abdul Kareem indicated, however, that the U.S. tendency to use its FTA with Singapore[35] as a model in other negotiations is causing problems in its talks with Malaysia.[36]

The Postponement of the Ninth Round of Talks

Plans to hold the ninth round of negotiations in late 2008 were postponed following the U.S. presidential elections. In July 2008, Minister Muhyiddin announced that the ninth round would be held in Kuala Lumpur in November 2008.[37] However, on November 7, 2008, Deputy Prime Minister Najib Razak said, "Malaysia was not able to conclude the FTA with the present U.S. administration," and that Malaysia will have to wait to see the policies of the new Obama Administration.[38] On November 26, 2008, Minister Muhyiddin told an audience of Malaysian manufacturers that he had been told by the U.S. government that it wanted to postpone further negotiations on the FTA until after the Obama Administration was in place.[39] On December 15, 2008, U.S. Ambassador Keith, stated that the United States was interested in concluding the FTA negotiations "as early as possible in the new administration."[40]

Israel's Military Operations in Gaza and the FTA Talks

As a predominantly Muslim nation, Malaysia has a long history of support for what it sees as the Palestinian peoples' struggle for freedom from Israeli oppression. The day after Israel began Operation Cast Lead, Malaysia's Prime Minister Abdullah Ahmad Badawi said in an official statement, "Malaysia deplores the disproportionate use of military power by Israel against the people of Gaza."[41] The following day, the Ministry of Foreign Affairs (MoFA) issued a statement that Malaysia "strongly condemns" Israel's military actions in Gaza asserting that "there is no excuse for the disproportionate, indiscriminate and excessive use of force in Gaza..."[42]

In the weeks following, popular opposition in Malaysia to Israel's military operations in Gaza grew and its focus spread to include the United States. Calls for a boycott of U.S. goods and services emerged from various sources within Malaysia, including former Prime Minister Mahathir Mohamad, members of parliament, political parties and public interest groups.[43] Specific U.S. boycott targets include Coca Cola, KFC, McDonalds, and Starbucks. There are also anti-boycott voices in Malaysia who claim that the boycott will hurt Malaysian-owned businesses and workers more than the parent U.S. companies.

On January 10, 2009, the Malaysian Bar Council urged a "review" of the FTA negotiations with the United States to protest what was seen as U.S. support for "Israeli atrocities against Palestinians."[44] Other groups also called for the suspension of FTA talks. Two days later, Minister Muhyiddin stated that the Ministry of International Trade and Industry (MITI) was suspending the FTA negotiations until it received orders and guidance from Malaysia's Cabinet.[45] There were indications that MITI's decision was at least partially in response to the events in Gaza. The next day, Prime Minister Badawi requested that Minister Muhyiddin formally brief the Cabinet of the decision to suspend the FTA talks.46 On January 15, 2009, Minister Muhyiddin indicated that the FTA negotiations had been postponed at the request of the United States until after the presidential inauguration. He also said in regards to the proposed boycott of U.S. products, "If there are any Malaysians who want to take such an action, it is their right. As for the government, we have not taken any decision on the matter."[47]

KEY ISSUES

Over the last three years, several issues have emerged as difficult topics in the negotiations. The main topics still to be resolved include intellectual property rights (IPR) protection, market access for U.S. automobiles and agricultural goods in Malaysia, trade in services, and government procurement policies.

Intellectual Property Rights

An issue of interest to many U.S. exporters, and in particular software and pharmaceutical companies, is Malaysian IPR regulations and enforcement.

Malaysia has recently tightened its laws on and stepped up enforcement of protection of intellectual property, but problems still remain. The Business Software Alliance (BSA) estimated 59% of the software in Malaysia in 2007 was pirated, resulting in industry losses of $311 million.[48]

Malaysia has remained on the Special 301 Watch List since October 2001 as part of an effort by the USTR to monitor Malaysia's efforts to improve its IPR regime. In its *2008 Special 301 Report*, the USTR stated that "Malaysia continued to show a strong commitment to strengthening IPR protection and enforcement this past year, but still needs to make further IPR improvements.[49] IPR enforcement improvements during 2007 included the creation of a specialized IPR court, which began hearing cases in 2007. The USTR also stated that it would be "pressing IPR issues through the ongoing U.S.-Malaysia Free Trade Agreement negotiations."[50]

With regard to IPR protection for pharmaceuticals, Malaysia is concerned about the U.S. preference for "TRIPs plus" provisions in the U.S.-Malaysia FTA.[51] The United States reportedly would like tighter restrictions on the use of compulsory licensing (CL) [52] and wishes to include data exclusivity provisions in the FTA.[53]

Malaysia is reluctant to accept terms that would undermine its ability to utilize the CL provisions of TRIPs for drugs deemed necessary to prevent the spread of an epidemic or avoid a national health emergecy. Opposition has appeared in Malaysia among people concerned about the treatment of HIV/AIDS. They claim that a U.S.-Malaysia FTA would more than likely patent anti-retroviral AIDS drugs for five years, "making [them] far too costly for them [HIV/AIDS patients] to buy."[54] Others believe that stricter enforcement of drug patents could discourage pharmaceutical companies from introducing new anti-retroviral drugs in Malaysia.[55] Malaysia has used the CL provisions of TRIPs to provide low-cost anti-retroviral drugs to HIV/AIDS patients in Malaysia.

Automobiles and Agricultural Goods

Malaysia has a growing automobile industry. For many years, the Malaysian government has promoted the development of a domestic automobile industry as a sign of its emergence as a modern industrial nation. Its automobile manufacturers, such as Proton and Perodua, market their vehicles in over 40 countries around the world, and its motorcycle manufacturer, Modenas, is a popular brand in Argentina, Greece, Iran,

Singapore, Malta, Mauritius, Turkey, and Vietnam. Malaysia's automobile components and parts industry is also quite successful on the world market.

Malaysia has long protected its automobile manufacturing industry from foreign competition using high tariffs and non-tariff trade barriers. Government policies also distinguish between national cars (i.e., made by domestic producers, such as Proton and Perodua) and non-national cars, which include most vehicles manufactured in Malaysia by non-Malaysian owned firms. The firms making national cars, for example, receive 50% rebates on their excise taxes. *Bumiputera* also are favored in receiving permits to import or distribute motor vehicles.

The government has, however, begun to dismantle some of its protections in order to meet its commitments to the WTO and the ASEAN Free Trade Agreement. In January 2004, the government completely eliminated local content requirements that were inconsistent with its obligations under the WTO, but government policies (particularly its excise taxes on automobiles) continue to block open trade in the automotive sector. Malaysia imposes 30% tariffs on assembled vehicles from outside the ASEAN region and up to 10% on completely knocked-down vehicle kits. Excise taxes on both assembled vehicles and kits are 80-200% on automobiles, 55- 160% on multipurpose vehicles, and 20-50% on motorcycles.[56]

During negotiations, Malaysia is likely to raise the issue of U.S. measures protecting its domestic automobile industry. For example, the United States currently maintains a special 25% tariff on imports of pickup trucks. At a May 2006 Trade Policy Staff Committee hearing, a representative of the U.S. Automotive Trade Policy Council (ATPC), which represents the U.S. big three automakers, said the Council supports the proposed FTA and sees it as an opportunity to break into a market that has historically protected domestic producers and discriminated against foreign manufacturers.[57]

From the outset of the negotiations, Malaysia has stated that rice was considered "strategic crop" and would not be included in the FTA and that tariffs on other agricultural goods (such as poultry) would not be lowered in order to protect its "farmers, planter, and fishermen." On November 13, 2008, Minister of Agriculture and Agro-based Industry Mustapa Mohamad said that Malaysia was "steadfast" in its decision to designate rice as a "strategic crop" that would not be included in any FTA with the United States. Malaysia has also expressed concerns about U.S. SPS regulations, which have been criticized by several nations as forming a non-tariff trade barrier.[58] The United States reportedly continues to press Malaysia to remove or reduce its restrictions on the trade of agricultural goods.

Trade in agricultural goods was reportedly discussed during the July 2008 talks, including SPS measures.

Trade in Services

Financial services also appear to be a difficult issue to resolve in the negotiations. Malaysia limits foreign ownership to 30% of commercial banks and 49% of investment banks. Foreign commercial banks also are allowed to open new branches only if they also add other branches as directed by Bank Negara, Malaysia's central bank. Malaysia maintains a 51% cap on foreign ownership of insurance companies already established in Malaysia prior to 1998 as well as a foreign ownership limit of 30% for new entrants seeking access. Malaysia has not enforced the 51% cap except in cases of companies who seek the right to establish branches.[59]

In the lead-up to the launch of the FTA negotiations, Malaysia reportedly attempted to keep financial services out of the negotiations completely, but the country did agree to include such services in the FTA talks. Malaysia, however, has lifted requirements that foreign banks obtain 50% of their credit from local banks, has allowed them to seek any amount of ringgit (the domestic currency) credit without approval, has allowed the ringgit exchange value to float rather than be strictly pegged to the dollar, and allowed foreign banks to open four additional branches in 2006.[60] However, the recent financial crisis in the United States has reignited concerns in Malaysia about the risks associated with greater foreign participation in its financial sector.

In telecommunications, foreign companies are allowed to acquire up to a 30% equity stake in existing fixed line operations. Value-added telecommunications service suppliers likewise are limited to 30% foreign equity. These restrictions arguably benefit the government-controlled firm, Telekom Malaysia.[61]

Licensed professionals, such as lawyers and architects, also are restricted in Malaysia. Foreign lawyers may not practice Malaysian law nor affiliate with local firms. Foreign law firms may take an operating stake of up to 30% in a local law firm. A foreign architectural firm may operate in Malaysia only as a joint venture participant in a specific project, and foreign architects may not be licensed in Malaysia. Foreign engineers may be licensed only for specific projects. Foreign accounting firms must work through Malaysian affiliates.[62]

In services, the United States has used the *negative list* approach in determining which sectors are excluded from the agreement.[63] Malaysia prefers to use a *positive list* approach in which service sectors are excluded unless listed in the agreement.

Government Procurement

Malaysia is not a signatory of the WTO Government Procurement Agreement. As part of its "New Economic Program," Malaysia seeks to raise the participation of *bumiputera* in the economy. Foreign companies, in many cases, are required to take on a local partner before their bids are considered. The awarding process for procurement contracts also is considered to be non-transparent.[64]

After the second round of negotiations in July 2006, it became apparent that Malaysian government procurement restrictions that reserve a certain share of Malaysian business for *bumiputera* were emerging as a major sticking point in the negotiations. Malaysian negotiators reportedly had not been authorized by the Malaysian Cabinet to agree to an opening of the government procurement market.[65]

In addition, there is strong interest in segments of the Malaysian business community to obtain preferential access to the U.S. government procurement process.[66] Tan Sri Yong, president of the Federation of Malaysian Manufacturers (FMM), commented, "At the moment, Malaysian companies cannot access the American government procurement, which is 65 times larger than ours. This means our furniture and computers cannot be supplied to the U.S. government."[67]

The United States has apparently offered limited access to its government procurement – the opportunity to bid on approximately $250 billion in contracts – to keep the comparative value of market access proportional. The Malaysia government procurement market has an estimated value of approximately $20 billion.

The government procurement issue was apparently not a major topic of negotations during the two rounds of talks held in 2008.Following the January 2008 round of negotiations, U.S. Assistant Trade Representative Weisel reported that the government procurement was not discussed because the Malaysian government was reviewing its position.[68]

INTERESTS, BENEFITS AND POTENTIAL OPPOSITION

The proposed U.S.-Malaysia FTA is of interest to Congress because: (1) it requires congressional approval; (2) it would continue the past trend toward greater trade liberalization and globalization; (3) it may include controversial provisions; and (4) it would affect certain trade flows that would, in turn, affect U.S. businesses or farmers, particularly import-competing industries and those exporting to Malaysia.

Among the initial responses to the USTR's 2006 FTA announcement were a statement by Senator Max Baucus welcoming the agreement, and statements by Representatives Jim Kolbe and Dan Burton hailing the launch of the negotiations.[69] The National Association of Manufacturers indicated that it has been a leading advocate of an FTA with Malaysia,[70] and a U.S.-Malaysia Free Trade Agreement (FTA) Business Coalition was organized on March 8, 2006.[71] Objections to the proposed FTA have come from some Malaysian and U.S. labor unions, farmers, fishermen and academics.[72]

Malaysia plays into U.S. interests through its economy and trade; its role in countering radical Islamic organizations; the example it sets as a democratic secular Muslim state; its position as a member of ASEAN, Asia Pacific Economic Cooperation (APEC), and other multilateral fora; its shared interest in dealing with a rising China; and the common goal of securing a safe shipping channel through the Strait of Malacca.[73]

A U.S.-Malaysia FTA was part of the Bush Administration's strategy to press for regional and bilateral trade initiatives in order to "ignite a new era of global economic growth through free markets and free trade."[74] In a broader sense, the proposed FTA would be a step toward realization of APEC's "Bogor Vision," under which the United States and APEC's other 21 members are working toward "free and open trade in the Pacific." At the 2006 APEC meetings, the United States proposed that APEC consider forming a Free Trade Area of the Asia Pacific that would accomplish this goal.[75] With the Doha Round of multilateral trade talks under the World Trade Organization (WTO) encountering problems, some see FTAs as a plausible alternative.

When announcing the proposed negotiations, the USTR listed four major goals associated with a U.S.-Malaysia FTA. These were: (1) to create new opportunities for U.S. manufacturers, farmers, and service providers; (2) to strengthen U.S. competitiveness and generate high-paying jobs; (3) to strengthen U.S. economic partnerships in the region; and (4) to advance broader U.S. strategic goals.[76] Other benefits mentioned for the proposed FTA included: (5) to cement a vibrant U.S.- Malaysia economic relationship; (6) to increase U.S. exports; (7) to diversify U.S. exports; (8) to increase investment; (9) to increase the sharing of knowledge and know-how between U.S. companies and Malaysian companies; (10) to enhance economic growth and job creation; and (11) to lower costs and create more competitive companies.[77]

In Malaysia, the Ministry of International Trade and is leading the negotiations. The Ministry lists as its FTA objectives to: (1) seek better market access for Malaysian goods and services; (2) further facilitate and promote bilateral trade and investment flows as well as economic development; (3) enhance the competitiveness of Malaysian producers and exporters through collaboration; and (4) build capacity in specific targeted areas thorough technical cooperation. The Ministry also views the proposed FTA as comprehensive and covering liberalization of the goods and services sector; trade and investment promotion and facilitation activities; investment protection; economic and technical cooperation programs; and having appropriate flexibility to facilitate development objectives.[78] The Ministry also noted that it would seek "flexibility and longer phase-in periods for sensitive sectors."[79]

Several Malaysian industries have been generally supportive of the proposed FTA, principally because they believe that they will benefit from greater access to the U.S. market. Among these industries are clothing and textiles, ceramics, lumber, rubber and consumer electronics. In addition, Malaysia hopes the FTA will increase inward foreign direct investment (FDI) from the United States and other nations because of Malaysia's improved access to the U.S. market.

A U.S.-Malaysia FTA would also improve U.S. access to the economies of Southeast Asia. Malaysia already has FTAs with Indonesia, Brunei, Singapore, the Philippines, and Vietnam under the ASEAN free trade area, and ASEAN is nearing completion of an FTA with India. It has FTAs with South Korea and Pakistan, an economic partnership agreement with Japan covering most goods trade, a partial FTA with China, and it is negotiating FTAs with Australia and New Zealand, and discussing an FTA with India. On April 19, 2007, Chile and Malaysia announced they would start negotiations on the establishment of a bilateral FTA in June, with the first round of talks held in Kuala Lumpur.[80]

When announcing the initiation of FTA negotiations, the USTR indicated that via the proposed FTA, the U.S. government is hoping to further build the broader relations with a country that has been on the "forefront of Asia's economic transformation and is a leader in the region and beyond." The USTR hoped that this FTA would strengthen U.S. cooperation with Malaysia in multilateral and regional fora, reinforce a strong U.S.-ASEAN relationship, and advance U.S. commercial and strategic interests in Asia.[81]

As a moderate, democratic Muslim nation, Malaysia plays a strategic role in U.S. foreign policy. In 2005, Prime Minister Abdullah urged Muslims around the world to guard against extremism and improve ties with the West while promoting his nation's moderate version of Islam.[82] The Bush Administration also hoped that the proposed FTA would reinforce the shared interests of the United States and Malaysia, promote common values, and facilitate cooperation in counterterrorism, defense, counter-narcotics, education, and in other areas.[83] Malaysia (along with Indonesia, Singapore, and Thailand) plays a key role in protecting vital maritime shipping lanes in the Strait of Malacca from pirates and terrorism.

In the United States, opposition to the proposed FTA has emerged from labor unions and environmental protection organizations, as well as "anti-globalization" groups. In Malaysia, voices opposing the FTA have arisen from labor unions, farmers, fishermen and other groups, as well as from opposition political parties. In some cases, opponents to a U.S.-Malaysia FTA from both nations have formed coalitions.[84]

With respect to labor interests, the AFL-CIO opposes additional FTAs unless they contain meaningful protections for workers' rights and environmental standards. Its position is that the Bush Administration launched or concluded bilateral free trade agreements that include no enforceable protections for core workers' rights, and move "backwards from previous accords on workers' rights, and contain many of the same flawed rules that have worsened our trade deficit" under the North American Free Trade Agreement (NAFTA).[85] Labor organizations also are interested in ensuring that labor laws in the bilateral trading partner country are brought up to International Labor Organization (ILO) standards and that a dispute settlement or enforcement mechanism is included in agreements that would preclude partner countries from reversing labor gains or weakening labor laws following congressional approval and implementation of their respective FTAs.[86] During the presidential campaign, Barack Obama expressed some support for the labor unions' concerns about the labor provisions of the negotiated FTAs with Colombia and South Korea.

Labor conditions in Malaysia have been the subject of some international criticism. According to Malaysian law, workers are afforded a variety of rights and most workers have the right to engage in trade union activity. However, according to the latest U.S. State Department country report on Malaysia, only 9.5% of the labor force was represented by trade unions.[87] In addition,

Malaysian trade union officials report extended delays of up to four years in obtaining legal recognition of their union. A specific area of international concern has been the working conditions of Malaysia's estimated 2.5 million immigrant workers—most from Indonesia—who reportedly face abuse and exploitation by employers and recruitment agencies.[88]

There has also been organized opposition to a U.S.-Malaysia FTA from Malaysians. On January 11, 2007, an anti-FTA campaign in northern Malaysia resulted in petitions with over 20,000 farmer and fishermen signatures being submitted to Malaysia's Prime Minister Abdullah and Malaysia's Ministry of International Trade and Industry. The petitions state that the proposed FTA would harm Malaysia's rice farmers and fishing industry.[89] In October 2006, a coalition of opposition parties, workers, and small businesses in Malaysia called for the cessation of negotiations with the United States until a study of the economic and social impact of the proposed FTA was conducted.[90]

Opposition to an FTA also may arise from various special interest groups. For example, Public Citizen, a nonprofit consumer advocacy organization in the United States, maintains that the FTA with Central America is "based on the same failed neoliberal NAFTA model, which has caused the 'race to the bottom' in labor and environmental standards and promotes privatization and deregulation of key public services."[91] In Malaysia, people concerned about the cost of pharmaceutical drugs, especially treatment for HIV/AIDS, are opposed to possible provisions in the FTA that they believe will raise the cost of prescription drugs in Malaysia.[92]

Another possible issue complicating the negotiations could be U.S. relations with Israel. Malaysia currently does not have diplomatic relations with Israel and requires export licenses for all goods sent to Israel. U.S. law currently contains several provisions designed to undermine official boycotts and trade embargoes aimed at Israel.[93] As previously mentioned, U.S. support for Israel's military operations in Gaza have given rise to a boycott of U.S. products and calls to suspend the FTA negotiations.

During recent congressional consideration of other proposed FTAs, opposition concerns have been addressed either in the implementing legislation or by securing various commitments in writing from the Administration. For example, in congressional consideration of the Dominican Republic-Central America-United States Free Trade Agreement (DR-CAFTA), the Bush Administration assuaged opposition from labor, sugar, and textile interests by promising certain actions to ameliorate adverse effects of the proposed FTA. In a letter, the Administration promised to allocate $40 million of FY2006 foreign operations appropriations for "labor and environmental enforcement capacity building assistance," and to continue to request this level of funding in budgets for fiscal years 2007 through 2009. The Bush Administration also stated that it would not allow the DR-CAFTA to interfere with the operation of the sugar program through FY2007 as the program is defined in the Farm Security and Rural Investment Act of 2002. For the textile and apparel industry, promises were made related to rules of origin, stricter customs enforcement with respect to Mexican inputs used in DR-CAFTA textile and apparel products, and actions to increase use of U.S. fabric.[94]

THE POTENTIAL EFFECTS OF A U.S.-MALAYSIA FTA

The usual goal of free trade agreements is to reduce barriers to trade and investment. In addition to eliminating or reducing tariffs on both sides, FTAs often eliminate or reduce import quotas and other non-tariff barriers to trade. They also usually provide access to services, open markets for investment, contain provisions strengthening protection of intellectual property, address certain types of government regulations and practices, provide for a dispute settlement process, and can touch on issues such as business visas, competition policy, and a variety of policies or practices that affect economic activity.

FTAs also create winners and losers. In general, the ones who gain from FTAs tend to be exporters, investors, and consumers, while those who lose tend to be companies and workers in import-competing industries. In addition, non-party countries could the FTA can be affected by the terms of the agreement, as trade is created or diverted between nations.[95]

An FTA with Malaysia would be the third FTA negotiation by the United States with a Southeast Asian nation, following the U.S.-Singapore FTA that came into effect on January 1, 2004, and a proposed U.S.-Thailand FTA whose negotiations are currently stalled. The United States also has an FTA with Australia and is negotiating an FTA with South Korea. On May 10, 2004, the United States and Malaysia signed a Trade and Investment Framework Agreement.[96]

Past FTAs negotiated by the United States usually provide for tariff free trade between the two countries with a phase-in period for sensitive sectors. With Malaysia, some trade already is tariff free. Both the United States and Malaysia participate in the Information Technology Agreement[97] (ITA) under which tariffs on semiconductors and other information technology products are bound at zero. The majority of current U.S. exports to Malaysia are covered by this agreement. Semiconductors and parts for computers alone account for more than half of U.S. exports to Malaysia. An FTA, however, would open markets artificially restricted by tariff and non-tariff barriers. Many of the more competitive U.S. exports face relatively high duties in Malaysia. These include products such as motor vehicles and parts, off-road dumpers, polyethylene, motorcycles, and adhesives.[98] For more information on the relative tariff rates of the two nations, see Appendix C.

The potential impact of an FTA depends on various other factors, including the relative size of the two nations, the amount and nature of their bilateral trade flows, the size of bilateral FDI in each nation, as well as existing trade relations with other nations. Below is a summary of key aspects of these factors.

THE MALAYSIAN ECONOMY

Table 1 provides a summary of Malaysia's key economic indicators. Malaysia has been one of the fastest growing economies in the world over the last few years. Early in 2008, Malaysia experienced a sharp rise in inflation, but the inflationary pressures subsided as the impact of the U.S. and E.U. economic slowdown affected Malaysia's exports. Malaysia's GDP and average per capita income make it a market considerably larger than most of the countries that have recently negotiated free trade agreements with the United States. At official exchange rates, the per capita income in 2007 was $6,724, but its purchasing power parity was estimated by the World Bank at $13,570 – higher than Argentina, Chile, and Mexico.[99]

Table 1. Selected Indicators for the Malaysian Economy

	2007	2008 (est.)	2009 (proj.)
Real GDP Growth	6.3%	6.3%	6.0%
Nominal GDP ($ billion)	186.7	223.7	209.9
Per Capita Income	$6,724	$7,898	$7,308
Inflation Rate - CPI	2.0%	5.5%	N.A.
Inflation Rate - PPI	6.7%	10.4%	N.A.
Unemployment Rate	3.2%	3.5%	3.2%
Exports ($ billion)	176.0	206.6	179.5
	146.9	170.5	155.2

Source: Malaysian Economy, Ministry of Finance, December 2008.

According to Malaysia's Ministry of Finance, the United States is its largest trading partner and largest foreign investor. According to U.S. trade figures, Malaysia was the tenth largest trading partner of the United States in 2007. The United States exported more to Malaysia in the first 11 months of 2008 than it did to Colombia or Peru, two other nations with pending FTAs with the United States. For the first 10 months of 2008, U.S. investment in Malaysia totaled $1.8 billion— the second greatest source of foreign investment in Malaysia, after Australia.[100]

BILATERAL TRADE FLOWS

FTAs usually have several distinct effects on trade flows. They tend to divert export and import trade toward the countries involved, but they also can create more trade overall by lowering tariffs and other trade barriers. FTAs also can cause a substitution effect as imports are substituted for domestic production. In that case, import-competing industries may suffer and may request assistance to adjust to increased competition from imports.

Merchandise Trade

. shows U.S. exports to, imports from, and the balance of merchandise trade with Malaysia from 2000 to 2007, according to the U.S. Department of Commerce and Malaysia's Department of Statistics. According to the United States, U.S. exports to Malaysia remained steady at about $10 billion per year from 2000 to 2005, but rose to over $12.5 billion in 2006 and then declined to $11.7 billion in 2007. U.S. imports from Malaysia grew from 2001 to 2006, but then declined in 2007. From 2001 to 2006, the U.S. bilateral trade deficit with Malaysia widened by 63.5%, but narrowed by 10.7% in 2007.

According to Malaysia, its exports to the United States rose from just over $20 billion in 2000 to about $30 billion in 2006—an increase of nearly 50%— and then slipped to $27.5 billion 2007. Over the same time period, Malaysia's imports from the United States rose 20% from $13.6 billion in 2000 to $16.4 billion in 2006 and then declined by nearly $500 million in 2007. Malaysia's resulting trade surplus with the United States was $6.5 billion in 2000 and $11.6 billion in 2006—roughly $8-$10 billion less than the U.S. figures. For more detailed information on U.S. trade with Malaysia, see Appendices D, E and F. As shown in Table 3. , the United States is Malaysia's top export market, according to Malaysian export data. Singapore is second, Japan is third, and China is fourth. Over the last three years, the portion of Malaysia's exports going to the United States has declined from 19.7% to 15.6%. China's share over the same period rose from 6.6% to 8.8%.

Table 2. U.S. Trade with Malaysia, 2000 to 2007
(Billion U.S. Dollars)

Year	U.S. Data			Malaysian Data		
	U.S. Exports	Malaysian Imports	Trade Balance	Malaysian Exports	U.S. Imports	Trade Balance
2000	10.957	25.568	-14.611	20.155	13.648	6.507
2001	9.358	22.340	-12.982	17.808	11.800	6.008
2002	10.344	24.009	-13.665	18.816	13.079	5.737
2003	10.914	25.440	-14.526	17.791	12.195	5.596
2004	10.922	28.179	-17.257	23.564	15.239	8.325
2005	10.461	33.685	-23.224	27.743	14.768	12.975
2006	12.544	36.533	-23.989	30.187	16.422	13.765
2007	11.680	32.629	-20.949	27.513	15.927	11.586

Table 3. Malaysia's Merchandise Exports by Top Five Trading Partners
(Billion U.S. Dollars)

Partner	2005	2006	2007
World Total	140.979	160.845	176.311
United States	27.743	30.187	27.513
Singapore	22.009	24.757	25.786
Japan	13.181	14.249	16.099
China	9.303	11.735	15.461
Thailand	7.585	8.506	8.735

Source: Department of Statistics, Malaysia via Global Trade Atlas.

As shown in Table 4, Japan has been and remains Malaysia's top source of imports, while the United States has slid from second to fourth since 2005. Over the last two years, both China and Singapore overtook the United States as a supplier of imported goods for Malaysia, with China edging close to Japan.

Table 4. Malaysia's Merchandise Imports by Top Five Trading Partners (Billion U.S. Dollars)

	2005	2006	2007
World Total Partner	114.626	131.223	147.065
Japan	16.634	17.347	19.096
China	13.177	15.896	18.919
Singapore	13.425	15.338	16.879
United States	14.768	16.422	15.927
Taiwan	6.331	7.161	8.354

Source: Department of Statistics, Malaysia via Global Trade Atlas.

In Asia, Malaysia already has FTAs with Japan and Singapore and is negotiating FTAs with Australia, India, New Zealand, and Pakistan. Meanwhile, China has signed an FTA with ASEAN, to which Malaysia is a member, which includes a trade in services agreement that went into force as of July 2007. The proposed FTA with the United States would place U.S. exporters on similar footing as exporters from China, Japan, and Singapore—Malaysia's other leading trading partners.

Trade in Services

According to current U.S. data, Malaysia is not and has not been a major services trading partner for the United States (see Table 5.). Total services trade with Malaysia amounted to less than $2 billion per year from 2000 to 2004, and just climbed above $2 billion in 2005. When compared to the total value of U.S. services trade, Malaysia's relatively small role in overall services trade becomes apparent. Even at its peak, Malaysia represented less than half a percent of the U.S. services export market and provided less than a third of a percent of the U.S. services imports.

Despite the relatively small current volume of services trade with Malaysia, several U.S. service sectors—including telecommunications, financial services, and insurance providers—have expressed strong interest in obtaining improved access to Malaysia's domestic market.

Table 5. U.S. Services Trade with Malaysia and the World
(Billion U.S. Dollars)

		2000	2001	2002	2003	2004	2005	2006	2007
Malaysia	Exports	1.118	1.193	1.167	1.218	1.187	1.438	1.623	1.890
	Imports	0.387	0.525	0.493	0.514	0.611	0.721	0.840	1.020
World	Exports	284.027	272.814	279.561	290.217	336.332	368.496	415.321	479.980
	Imports	207.392	204.074	209.048	221.938	258.147	279.486	313.865	341.126
Malaysia's Share	Exports	0.394%	0.437%	0.417%	0.420%	0.353%	0.390%	0.391%	0.39
	Imports	0.187%	0.257%	0.236%	0.232%	0.237%	0.258%	0.268%	0.29

Source: U.S. Bureau of Economic Analysis.

The United States already is Malaysia's top export market for merchandise goods. A U.S.- Malaysia FTA would likely reinforce this relationship. Similarly, the discussed FTA would offer better access to U.S. services providers to Malaysia's domestic market.

U.S. Investment in Malaysia

According to the U.S. Bureau of Economic Analysis, U.S. companies by 2007 had invested over $15 billion in Malaysia (see Table 6.). About 38% of U.S. investments in Malaysia was in the manufacturing sector, with investments in computer and electronic equipment manufacturing facilities accounting for over three-quarters of the manufacturing investments. Also within manufacturing investments, U.S. companies have shown a growing interest in chemical manufacturing operations in Malaysia.

Table 6. U.S. Foreign Direct Investment in Malaysia, 2000-2007 (Million U.S. Dollars)

Year	TOTAL	Manufacturing - Total	Manufacturing - Computers and Electronic Equipment	Manufacturing - Chemical
2000	7,910	5,028	4,385	250
2001	7,489	5,006	4,322	203
2002	7,101	3,060	2,370	195
2003	7,057	3,213	2,404	255
2004	8,909	4,075	2,801	720
2005	11,097	4,670	3,316	791
2006	12,557	4,581	3,130	839
2007	99	3	1	889

Source: U.S. Bureau of Economic Analysis.

According to the Malaysian Industrial Development Authority (MIDA), U.S. companies obtained approval for 33 manufacturing projects worth $878 million in 2007 and 19 projects worth $1.8 billion in the first 10 months of 2008. MIDA reported that most of the U.S. investment has been in the electronic equipment industry and the chemical industry, indicating a continued focus of U.S. investors in those two sectors.

ISSUES FOR THE 111TH CONGRESS

When the talks began, the USTR's goal was to have the U.S.-Malaysia FTA implementing bill considered by Congress under "fast track" expedited procedures of the Bipartisan Trade Promotion Authority (TPA) Act of 2002 (P.L. 107-210).[101] However, the statute requires the President to notify Congress of his intention to enter into the agreement at least 90 calendar days before entering into the trade agreement. Since the President's Trade Promotion Authority expired on July 1, 2007, and the President did not notify the Congress by the April 2, 2007 deadline, the U.S.-Malaysia FTA became ineligible to be considered under the 2002 TPA.

As a result, there are several possible scenarios under which a proposed FTA with Malaysia might be considered by Congress. First, if Congress were to extend, renew or revise Trade Promotion Authority, then the U.S.-Malaysia FTA might be considered under the provisions of a new TPA law. Second, Congress could choose to pass legislation providing temporary or limited TPA for the proposed U.S.-Malaysia FTA. This approach was used when Congress considered the Uruguay Round Agreements. Third, Congress could consider the proposed U.S.-Malaysia FTA without TPA, as it did with the U.S.-Jordan FTA. However, consideration of the proposed FTA with Malaysia without TPA would potentially allow Congress to amend the implementing bill in ways that could modify the terms of the trade agreement.

In the meantime, while negotiations with Malaysia on the proposed FTA are incomplete, the legislative policy options include consultations with the Executive Branch, holding oversight hearings on pertinent U.S. trade policy and relations with Malaysia and other nations, and working with interest groups that either support or oppose the proposed agreement. P.L. 107-210 (Section 2104) provides for close consultations with the Executive Branch during and following the negotiations. Such consultations could lead to changes in the draft agreement before it is signed.

APPENDIX A. MAP OF MALAYSIA

Source: Map Resources. Adapted by CRS.

APPENDIX B. CHRONOLOGY[102]

2008	
July 14-18	Eighth Round of Talks held in Washington, DC
January 14	Seventh Round of Talks held in Kuala Lumpur, Malaysia
2007	
April 13	Informal Sixth Round of Talks held in Washington, DC.
March 7	Malaysian Cabinet meet to discuss 58 outstanding issues in the FTA negotiations.
February 5	Fifth Round of Talks begin in Kota Kinabalu, Sabah, Malaysia.
January 8	Fourth Round of Talks begin in San Francisco.
2006	
December 27	The Administration reports that it is not likely to ask Congress to substantially change U.S. import laws (trade remedies laws) due to negotiations on a free trade agreement with Malaysia.
October 30	Third Round of Talks commences in Malaysia. Government procurement is a major point of contention.
September 18	Third Round of Talks scheduled for September are postponed to October 30.

Appendix B. (Continued)

July 17-21	The Second Round of Talks is held. Twenty-two negotiating groups met and discussed issues and draft texts.
June 12-14	The First Round of the Malaysia-US FTA Talks are held in Malaysia.
May 3	The interagency Trade Policy Staff Committee convenes a public hearing to seek public comment to assist the USTR in amplifying and clarifying negotiating objectives for the proposed U.S.-Malaysia FTA and to provide advice on how specific goods and services and other matters should be treated under the proposed agreement. The U.S. International Trade Commission began hearings on the proposed U.S. Malaysia FTA.
April 4	The U.S. Trade Representative sends a letter to the Committee on Ways and Mea transmitting a report on the intent to initiate negotiations for a free trade agreement between the United States and Malaysia.
March 31	The Trade Policy Staff Committee gives notice that the U.S. Trade Representative and the Department of Labor are initiating a review of the impact of a proposed free trade agreement between the United States and Malaysia on U.S. employment, including labor markets.
March 30	The U.S. International Trade Commission announces that it instituted (as of March 24) investigation [Nos. TA-131-33 and TA-2104-22] entitled U.S.-Malaysia Free Trade Agreement: Advice Concerning the Probable Economic Effect of Providing Duty-Free Treatment for Imports. The request for the investigation was received from the USTR on March 17, 2006.
March 8	The U.S. Trade Representative announces and notifies Congress of the Bush Administration's intent to negotiate a free trade agreement between the United

APPENDIX C. A COMPARISON OF U.S. AND MALAYSIAN TARIFF RATES

Measuring the degree of protection provided by tariff barriers is a complicated process, since each country has thousands of products each with a tariff rate that depends on the category of exporter. Average rates, therefore, will differ depending on how they are calculated. The two types of averages most often cited are the most favored nation (MFN) rates and the average applied rates.

Average MFN Tariff Rates

The MFN rates apply to most countries and all members of the World Trade Organization. U.S. exporters face these rates unless they have been reduced by a special arrangement, such as the Generalized System of Preferences[103] or the Information Technology Agreement. The average MFN rates are simple averages of all tariff lines. On an MFN basis, Malaysia's average tariff rate at 8.1% is higher than the 4.8% of the United States . shows the average and range of U.S. and Malaysian MFN tariff rates by major commodity category as classified under the Harmonized System.[104] Both the United States and Malaysia have peaks in tariff rates on certain products.

Malaysia and the United States each protects its agricultural sector. Although Malaysia's average MFN tariff rate for agricultural products at 3.2% is lower than the 9.7% of the United States, Malaysia maintains high rates on items of interest to U.S. agriculture. The Malaysian tariff rate for grains averages 15.2% and rice is at 40%, oranges and apples at 15% to 20%, and wheat flour at 96%. Prepared food is subject to tariffs of 5% to 30%. Beef enters the country at 15%, but pork faces a 139% tariff and ham 168%. The tariff is 25% on yogurt, 10 to 25% on chocolate products, and 20% on baby food. For the United States, the upper range for agricultural products is a 350% tariff on imports of tobacco products that exceed the import quota. Tobacco products within the quota face a 12.1% tariff rate. In recent years, the tobacco quota has not been filled, so the 350% rate has not been applied.

In non-agricultural products (excluding petroleum), Malaysia's average MFN tariff rate is 8.7% as compared with 4.0% in the United States. The ranges of tariff rates are similar. In Malaysian sectors where the government is fostering the growth of industry, however, the rates are particularly high. For transport equipment, the average Malaysia tariff of 25.6% is more than ten times the U.S. rate of 2.5%. For non-electrical machinery, a sector in which both countries currently export to each other, the Malaysia tariff rate at 6.3% is over four times the U.S. rate of 1.4%. Similarly, in electrical machinery the Malaysia rate of 9.2% is much higher the U.S. rate of 2.2%.

Table C-1. Average and Range of Malaysian and U.S. Most Favored Nation Tariff Rates

	Malaysia's Tariff Rates (2006)			U.S. Tariff Rates (2004)		
	No. of Lines	Average (%)	Range (%)	No. of Lines	Average (%)	Range (%)
Total	10,581	8.1	0-60	10,253	4.8	0-350
Agricultural products	1,202	3.2	0-40	1,595	8.9	0-350
Live animals and products thereof	142	0.8	0-20	139	4.2	0-100
Dairy products	40	6.1	0-25	166	21.4	0-177.2
Coffee and tea, cocoa, sugar, etc.	209	4.1	0-25	315	9.7	0-90.7
Cut flowers and plants	46	0.0	0-0	57	1.7	
Fruit and vegetables	302	3.9	0-30	439	6.3	0-13
Grains	21	15.2	0-40	21	1.6	
Oils seeds, fats, oil and their products	197	2.0	0-20	95	6.3	0-16
Beverages and spirits	81	6.4	0-30	100	4.8	0-15
Tobacco	19	5.0	5-5	47	56.0	0-35
Other agricultural products, n.e.s.	145	1.3	0-25	216	2.0	
Non-agricultural products (excl. petrol.)	9,349	8.7	0-60	8,658	4.0	
Fish and fishery products	188	3.2	0-20	201	2.0	

	Malaysia's Tariff Rates (2006)			U.S. Tariff Rates (2004)		
	No. of Lines	Average (%)	Range (%)	No. of Lines	Average (%)	Range (%)
Mineral products, precious stones, etc.	416	10.4	0-60	540	3.5	
Metals	1,061	17.5	0-50	1,015	1.9	
Chemicals and photographic supplies	1,481	5.1	0-50	1,833	3.7	
Leather, rubber, footwear, travel goods	397	13.1	0-40	397	7.3	
Wood, pulp, paper and furniture	2,370	2.5	0-40	526	0.7	
Textiles and clothing	1,176	12.6	0-30	1,659	9.1	
Transport equipment	461	25.8	0-50	242	2.5	
Non-electric machinery	735	6.3	0-35	790	1.4	
Electric machinery	438	9.5	0-50	529	2.2	
Non-agric products, n.e.s.	626	6.3	0-50	888	3.0	
Petroleum	30	0.5	0-5	28	2.2	
By sector a						
-Agriculture and fisheries	1,655	0.4	0-40	488	5.5	0-35
-Mining	124	1.0	0-30	116	0.3	
-Manufacturing	8,801	9.6	0-60	9,648	4.8	0-35

Table C-1. (Continued)

	Malaysia's Tariff Rates (2006)			U.S. Tariff Rates (2004)		
	No. of Lines	Average (%)	Range (%)	No. of Lines	Average (%)	Range (%)
-excluding food processing	7,904	10.2	0-60			
By stage of processing						
First stage of processing	2,054	0.9	0-40	959	3.7	0-35
Semi-processed products	3,482	9	0-60	3,418	4.2	
Fully-processed products	5	10.4	0-60	6	5.3	0-35

Source: World Trade Organization calculations, based on data provided by the Malaysian and U.S. authorities. See Trade Policy Review-Report by Malaysia, VVT/TPR/G/I 56, December 12, 2005, and Trade Policy Review-Report by the United States, VVT/TPR/S/200, June 9 & 11, 2008.

Note: Calculations exclude specific rates and include the ad valorem part of alternate and compound rates. The tariff is based on HS02 nomenclature. The number of lines refers to the number of individual lines in the list of tariffs for each country.

[a] International Standard Industrial (Rev.2) classification. Electricity, gas, and water are excluded.

Average Applied Tariff Rates

Applied average tariff rates are derived by dividing the amount of customs duties collected by the value of imports. Average applied tariff rates are frequently used indicators of a nation's actual level of tariff protection. These rates may be somewhat lower than the MFN rates because items with high rates might not be imported at all (so no tariffs are paid) and because a nation may have special trade arrangements with other nations under which the partners pay lower or no tariffs on their exports. They can also be higher if importers buy expensive items (such as machinery or automobiles) subject to higher tariff rates.

Table C-2. U.S. and Malaysian Average Applied Tariffs Rates for Industrial Goods - 2006

Industrial Category	Malaysia	United States
All Industrial Goods	9.1%	3.7%
Wood, pulp, paper, and furniture	10.9%	0.7%
Textiles and clothing	13.5%	9.6%
Leather, rubber, footwear, and travel goods	14.0%	4.3%
Metals	9.3%	2.1%
Chemicals and photographic supplies	3.6%	3.4%
Transport equipment	18.5%	3.2%
Non-electric machinery	3.7%	1.2%
Electric machine	6.7%	1.9%
Mineral products and precious stones	8.8%	2.0%
Manufactured articles not specified	5.1%	2.5%
Fish and fish	2.4%	1.1%

Source: U.S. Trade Representative. "Free Trade Agreement: U.S. and Malaysia, Economic and Strategic Benefits," March 8, 2006.

For Malaysia, the average applied tariff rate of 8.4% in 2006 was more than twice the U.S. average rate of 3.7%.[105] For all industrial goods, the applied rate is 9.1% in Malaysia as compared with 3.7% in the United States . shows Malaysian applied tariff rates for selected industrial sectors.

Appendix D. U.S. Merchandise Exports to Malaysia by Two-Digit Harmonized System Codes, 2005-2007
(US$ Million; FAS value)

	Description	2005	2006	2007
	Total Exports to Malaysia	10,450.9	12,550.1	11,680.2
01	Live Animals	2.3	2.4	3.6
02	Meat	3.3	2.0	3.8
03	Fish and Seafood	3.0	6.0	8.6
04	Dairy, Eggs, Honey, etc.	33.5	48.7	96.4
05	Other of Animal Origin	0.2	0.3	0.5
06	Live Trees and Plants	0.0	0.0	0.0
07	Vegetables	5.5	6.2	7.3
08	Edible Fruit and Nuts	117.6	94.3	57.4
09	Spices, Coffee and Tea	0.8	0.8	0.4
10	Cereals	29.8	23.5	76.3
11	Milling; Malt; Starch	1.5	1.6	2.2
12	Misc Grain, Seed, Fruit	26.2	58.8	119.5
13	Lac; Vegetable Sap, Extract	2.1	1.9	3.5
14	Other Vegetable	0.0	0.0	0.1
15	Fats and Oils	1.7	2.6	2.1
16	Prepared Meat, Fish, etc	1.0	0.8	1.7
17	Sugars	7.2	9.6	13.1
18	Cocoa	4.9	3.3	3.7
19	Baking Related	5.2	4.5	4.9
20	Preserved Food	23.2	24.3	32.6
21	Miscellaneous Food	46.7	48.8	52.6
22	Beverages	4.0	5.8	8.5
	Description	2005	2006	2007
23	Food Waste; Animal Feed	37.2	39.2	45.5
24	Tobacco	27.9	21.1	14.3
25	Salt; Sulfur; Earth, Stone	4.5	8.7	8.1
26	Ores, Slag, Ash	4.0	5.0	5.0
27	Mineral Fuel, Oil Etc.	30.3	42.6	55.3
28	Inorg Chem; Rare Earth mt	61.9	73.5	77.5
29	Organic Chemicals	113.1	107.0	121.2
30	Pharmaceutical Products	29.9	39.4	31.8
31	Fertilizers	6.0	5.5	
32	Tanning, Dye, Paint, Putty	20.3	17.2	
33	Perfumery, Cosmetic, etc	29.7	37.0	
34	Soap, Wax, Etc; Dental Prep	27.7	32.6	
35	Albumins; Mod Starch; Glue	8.0	10.7	
36	Explosives	3.6	3.7	
37	Photographic/Cinematography	4.6	4.2	

38	Misc. Chemical Products	76.8	73.8	115.
39	Plastic	222.2	208.4	230.
40	Rubber	34.1	45.4	
41	Hides and Skins	0.1	0.1	
42	Leather Art; Saddlery; Bags	2.6	3.0	
43	Furskin+ Artificial Fur	0.0	0.0	
44	Wood	30.1	29.7	
45	Cork	0.1	0.0	
46	Straw, Esparto	0.0	0.0	
47	Woodpulp, Etc.	26.4	28.1	
48	Paper, Paperboard	71.7	67.5	
49	Book+ Newspaper; Manuscript	20.1	18.3	
50	Silk; Silk Yarn, Fabric	0.3	0.5	
51	Animal Hair+ Yarn, Fabric	0.0	0.0	
52	Cotton+ Yarn, Fabric	5.4	8.5	
53	Other Vegetable Textile Fiber	0.0	0.0	
54	Manmade Filament, Fabric	4.0	2.8	
55	Manmade Staple Fibers	2.5	2.9	
56	Wadding, Felt, Twine, Rope	14.7	7.0	
57	Textile Floor Coverings	0.2	0.5	
58	Special Woven Fabric, Etc	0.5	1.0	
59	Impregnated Text Fabrics	3.9	2.9	
60	Knit, Crocheted Fabrics	0.3	0.1	
61	Knit Apparel	0.8	0.3	
62	Woven Apparel	2.4	1.4	
63	Misc Textile Articles	7.0	9.6	
64	Footwear	0.8	0.7	
65	Headgear	0.3	0.3	
66	Umbrella, Walking-sticks, Etc	0.0	0.0	
67	Artificial Flowers, Feathers	0.0	0.0	
68	Stone, Plaster, Cement, Etc	11.7	16.4	
69	Ceramic Products	9.5	4.3	
70	Glass and Glassware	27.0	30.4	
71	Precious Stones, Metals	37.1	48.9	
72	Iron and Steel	121.3	211.8	411.
73	Iron/steel Products	28.0	33.0	
74	Copper+ Articles Thereof	27.4	30.0	
75	Nickel+ Articles Thereof	3.0	4.0	
76	Aluminum	43.5	43.4	
78	Lead	4.4	3.0	
79	Zinc+articles Thereof	0.6	1.8	
80	Tin + Articles Thereof	0.1	6.8	
81	Other Base Metals, etc.	7.8	17.0	

Appendix D. (Continued)

	Description	2005	2006	2007
82	Tools, Cutlery, of Base Metals	22.5	28.3	
83	Misc Art of Base Metal	8.6	10.0	
84	Machinery	1,744.8	1,687.3	1,70
85	Electrical Machinery	5,985.7	7,131.2	6,32
86	Railway; Trf Sign eq	5.5	3.4	
87	Vehicles, Not Railway	15.8	13.7	
88	Aircraft, Spacecraft	255.8	807.3	320.
	Description	2005	2006	2007
89	Ships and Boats	10.5	1.2	
90	Optic, not 8544; Medical Instr	567.8	834.5	690.
91	Clocks and Watches	1.3	0.9	
92	Musical Instruments	1.2	1.9	
93	Arms and Ammunition	1.3	2.2	
94	Furniture and Bedding	29.8	13.7	
95	Toys and Sports Equipment	19.2	19.6	
96	Miscellaneous Manufactures	2.5	6.3	
97	Art and Antiques	0.2	0.4	
98	Other	201.4	231.2	226.

Source of data: U.S. International Trade Commission.

Appendix E. U.S. Merchandise Imports from Malaysia by Two-Digit Harmonized System Codes, 2005-2007
(U.S.$ Millions, CIF values)

HS	Description	2005	2006	2007
	Total Imports from Malaysia	34,675.8	37,521.1	32,628.5
01	Live Animals	0.2	0.1	0.2
02	Meat	0.0	0.0	0.0
03	Fish and Seafood	130.2	152.5	142.3
04	Dairy, Eggs, Honey, etc	0.8	0.3	2.7
05	Other of Animal Origin	0.1	0.1	0.1
06	Live Trees and Plants	0.8	0.8	0.7
07	Vegetables	0.3	0.1	0.0
08	Edible Fruit and Nuts	0.0	0.0	0.0
09	Spices, Coffee and Tea	1.8	3.6	3.8
10	Cereals	0.0	0.1	0.0
11	Milling; Malt; Starch	0.2	0.0	0.1
12	Misc. Grain, Seed, Fruit	0.2	0.3	0.0
13	Lac; Vegetable Sap, Extract	0.2	0.3	0.3
14	Other Vegetable	0.0	0.0	0.0

15	Fats and Oils	343.3	458.0	679.4
16	Prepared Meat, Fish, etc	18.3	21.7	34.5
17	Sugars	1.1	0.7	1.2
18	Cocoa	117.6	113.8	121.4
19	Baking Related	11.1	11.5	11.7
20	Preserved Food	9.4	8.4	10.2
21	Miscellaneous Food	9.6	22.7	39.7
22	Beverages	4.2	6.7	3.2
23	Food Waste; Animal Feed	0.7	4.2	7.4
24	Tobacco	1.0	0.0	0.0
25	Salt; Sulfur; Earth, Stone	0.2	0.2	0.1
26	Ores, Slag, Ash	9.5	10.7	8.2
27	Mineral Fuel, Oil Etc	549.7	457.8	424.6
28	Inorg Chem; Rare Earth mt	14.6	3.7	8.1
29	Organic Chemicals	108.0	94.5	109.3
30	Pharmaceutical Products	1.1	2.8	3.3
31	Fertilizers	13.4	14.7	16.4
32	Tanning, Dye, Paint, Putty	17.7	14.7	13.1
33	Perfumery, Cosmetic, etc	3.9	4.5	5.6
34	Soap, Wax, Etc; Dental Prep	21.6	25.3	23.8
35	Albumins; Mod Starch; Glue	0.7	0.6	0.4
36	Explosives	0.0	0.0	0.0
37	Photographic/Cinematography	1.5	3.3	0.7
38	Misc. Chemical Products	184.7	218.1	304.7
39	Plastic	153.3	187.6	162.8
40	Rubber	728.8	866.0	839.2
41	Hides and Skins	0.1	0.3	0.4
42	Leather Art; Saddlery; Bags	5.5	12.0	11.1
43	Furskin+ Artificial Fur	0.0	0.0	0.0
44	Wood	402.0	433.5	339.9
45	Cork	0.0	0.0	0.1
46	Straw, Esparto	0.2	0.0	0.0
47	Woodpulp, Etc.	0.0	0.0	0.0
48	Paper, Paperboard	19.4	19.8	27.9
49	Book+ Newspaper; Manuscript	22.5	21.9	26.7
50	Silk; Silk Yarn, Fabric	0.0	0.0	0.0
51	Animal Hair+ Yarn, Fabric	0.6	0.3	0.4
52	Cotton+ Yarn, Fabric	13.1	11.9	3.5
53	Other Vegetable Textile Fiber	0.0	0.0	0.0
54	Manmade Filament, Fabric	18.0	18.4	19.0
55	Manmade Staple Fibers	3.2	11.0	7.4
56	Wadding, Felt, Twine, Rope	12.5	12.5	9.1
57	Textile Floor Coverings	0.1	0.2	0.0
58	Special Woven Fabric, Etc	2.2	3.3	1.3

Appendix E. (Continued)

HS	Description	2005	2006	2007
59	Impregnated Text Fabrics	0.6	0.6	0.6
60	Knit, Crocheted Fabrics	0.0	0.1	0.2
61	Knit Apparel	462.2	459.2	447.2
62	Woven Apparel	274.7	283.4	255.6
63	Misc Textile Articles	8.3	6.0	6.3
64	Footwear	1.8	2.7	2.6
65	Headgear	3.5	3.1	2.4
66	Umbrella, Walking-sticks, Etc	0.0	0.0	0.0
67	Artificial Flowers, Feathers	0.0	0.0	0.0
HS	Description	2005	2006	2007
68	Stone, Plaster, Cement, Etc	5.3	2.8	6.3
69	Ceramic Products	38.1	36.8	27.8
70	Glass and Glassware	6.8	9.8	9.7
71	Precious Stones, Metals	30.3	30.5	23.7
72	Iron and Steel	143.7	323.5	159.0
73	Iron/steel Products	88.2	123.8	123.2
74	Copper+ Articles Thereof	57.5	107.3	123.1
75	Nickel+ Articles Thereof	0.0	0.4	0.7
76	Aluminum	54.5	38.4	33.6
78	Lead	0.0	0.0	0.0
79	Zinc+articles Thereof	1.6	1.0	0.7
80	Tin + Articles Thereof	16.3	4.3	2.2
81	Other Base Metals, etc.	0.0	2.2	0.3
82	Tools, Cutlery, of Base Metals	5.7	5.1	8.1
83	Misc Art of Base Metal	23.0	22.5	25.1
84	Machinery	13,130.8	15,229.2	14,347.9
85	Electrical Machinery	15,050.6	14,927.4	10,940.7
86	Railway; Trf Sign eq	0.4	0.9	0.5
87	Vehicles, Not Railway	30.2	32.6	33.9
88	Aircraft, Spacecraft	21.2	27.8	37.1
89	Ships and Boats	20.7	30.3	19.5
90	Optic, not 8544; Medical Instr	630.8	781.9	957.8
91	Clocks and Watches	7.0	1.9	1.6
92	Musical Instruments	2.3	2.0	2.2
93	Arms and Ammunition	0.4	0.5	0.5
94	Furniture and Bedding	914.7	993.8	829.7
95	Toys and Sports Equipment	109.9	96.8	95.0
96	Miscellaneous Manufactures	26.1	26.4	19.5
97	Art and Antiques	0.2	0.5	0.3
98	Special Other	301.4	376.2	412.9
99	Other Special Impr Provisions	247.9	273.6	244.9

Source of data: U.S. International Trade Commission.

APPENDIX F. U.S. MERCHANDISE EXPORTS
by State to Malaysia, 2004-2006
(U.S. Dollars)

State	2005	2006	2007
U.S. Total	10,460,833,167	12,544,269,310	11,680,201,598
Alabama	24,435,439	32,055,731	40,770,615
Alaska	1,813,626	2,110,093	3,348,500
Arizona	778,629,396	807,955,375	539,240,114
Arkansas	12,036,780	12,353,817	18,627,221
California	1,943,023,872	2,512,950,444	2,206,103,264
Colorado	246,103,616	242,375,536	206,722,451
Connecticut	115,115,730	155,261,689	204,818,869
Delaware	12,072,472	12,631,167	12,246,911
District of Columbia	6,053,657	4,385,022	4,923,895
Florida	231,852,408	173,138,280	174,820,666
Georgia	84,644,356	63,846,193	110,886,796
Hawaii	7,930,844	8,729,921	15,738,207
Idaho	150,111,154	152,678,546	124,308,415
Illinois	233,327,516	321,290,525	335,160,263
Indiana	75,658,664	84,684,105	112,639,142
Iowa	34,433,982	36,166,670	42,070,562
Kansas	43,925,781	31,365,428	34,254,656
Kentucky	105,575,397	104,453,457	178,508,976
Louisiana	98,810,927	93,280,926	219,286,946
Maine	364,620,488	673,323,738	723,770,235
Maryland	20,553,856	21,151,523	25,459,669
Massachusetts	617,627,876	535,218,544	521,805,171
Michigan	77,665,312	61,516,319	69,402,444
Minnesota	185,472,723	188,188,446	185,374,766
Mississippi	7,761,611	9,551,863	13,308,966
Missouri	53,093,743	49,591,784	43,202,476
Montana	7,295,218	5,299,170	4,377,357
Nebraska	7,694,801	10,251,464	13,227,045
Nevada	36,542,586	67,638,870	37,579,984
New Hampshire	23,779,985	31,678,258	22,499,579
New Jers	27	64	07 8
New Mexico	342,690,777	490,070,276	477,400,89
New York	239,245,648	261,717,799	322,290,70
North Carolina	182,575,269	141,852,400	108,657,72
North Dakota	1,042,341	835,254	2,240,58

Appendix F. (Continued)

State	2005	2006	2007
Ohio	119,261,745	83,616,979	112,772,99
Oklahoma	16,758,186	14,238,542	20,995,3
Oregon	914,985,840	1,215,312,164	1,076,571,89
Pennsylvania	169,575,146	181,442,354	188,153,31
Puerto Rico	23,768,292	16,792,176	12,282,1
Rhode Island	15,174,078	10,424,503	7,425,64
South Carolina	71,623,429	67,769,659	85,415,2
South Dakota	6,527,987	4,783,698	4,821,83
Tennessee	128,517,281	165,627,371	164,562,01
Texas	1,755,450,547	1,952,913,193	1,734,022,47
Utah	152,665,498	175,923,709	159,118,22
Vermont	49,582,756	29,682,822	40,571,5
Virgin Islands	123,452,142	189,635,487	242,587,65
Virginia	120,041	6,680,464	40,347
Washington	86,315,944	57,529,454	66,446,859
West Virginia	213,893,793	757,660,121	333,733,049
Wisconsin	23,128,249	8,463,557	22,153,272
State	2005	2006	2007
Wyoming	119,236,465 70	127,042,669 91	122,019,58
Unallocated			

Source: World Trade Atlas.

End Notes

[1] Office of the United States Trade Representative, "United States, Malaysia Announce Intention to Negotiate Free Trade Agreement," press release, March 8, 2006.

[2] "Remarks by United States Trade Representative Rob Portman and Malaysian Minister for Trade Rafidah Aziz at the Launch of U.S.—Malaysia Free Trade Negotiations," March 8, 2007, see U.S. Trade Representative webpage—
http://www.ustr.gov/assets—for transcript.

[3] Supporters of the U.S. boycott and the suspension of the FTA talks include some members of Malaysia's parliament, the Malaysian Bar Council, and the Malaysian Alliance of NGOs Against Oppression of Palestinians.

[4] *Bumiputera* (also *bumiputra*), is a Malay term (From Sanskrit, *bhumiputra*, "sons of the earth") referring to ethnic Malays as well as other indigenous ethnic groups, such as the Orang Asli in Peninsular Malaysia and the tribal peoples in Sabah and Sarawak. Malaysia's ethnic Chinese and Indian population are not considered *bumiputera*.

[5] "US Hopes to Conclude MUSFTA Talks Very Soon," *Nanyang Daily*, December 15, 2008.

[6] Jane Ritikos, "Malaysia Moving Forward in FTA Talks with US," *The Star*, October 2, 2008.

[7] Mohamad Idris, "Malaysia-US FTA—Stop Negotiations Immediately," *Malaysiakini*, July 15, 2008.
[8] "MITI Opened to Proposal for a White Paper on US-Malaysia FTA," *Bernama*, November 19, 2008.
[9] For more information on Israel's military operations in Gaza, see CRS Report R40101, *Israel and Hamas: Conflict in Gaza (2008-2009)*, coordinated by Jim Zanotti
[10] "PM to Muhyiddin: Explain Statement on Suspension of FTA Talks with US," *The Malaysian Insider*, January 13, 2009.
[11] In Malaysian culture, a person is often referred to in formal situations not by their surname, but by one of their given names. This report will follow this convention.
[12] "Rundingan FTA Dengan AS Dihentikan Sementara," *Utasan (in Malay)*, January 12, 2009; translation provided by U.S. Embassy in Kuala Lumpur.
[13] "FTA Talks between Malaysia and US to Resume in January 2009," *The Star*, November 27, 2008.
[14] The Office of the President-Elect, "More Members of the Economic Team," press release, December 19, 2008.
[15] Oorrjitham, op cit.
[16] Rupa Damodaran, Malaysia-US FTA Talks to Resume on January 14," *Business Times*, December 30, 2007.
[17] Ibid.
[18] "After 1-year Hiatus, Malaysia and US Resume FTA Talks," *The Times of India*, January 14, 2008.
[19] Kevin Tan, "US Hopeful of FTA with M'sia by Mid-year," *The Edge Daily*, January 24, 2008.
[20] "U.S., Malaysia Make Progress in Trade Talks," *Xinhua*, January 18, 2008.
[21] Ibid.
[22] "US Aims to Conclude FTA by Summer, Insists on Government Procurement," *Bernama*, January 17, 2008.
[23] Anna Maria Samsuddin, "US, Malaysia Make Progress in Trade Talks: Weisel," *New Strait Times*, January 18, 2008.
[24] "No Need for Deadline to Conclude Malaysia-US FTA, Says Rafidah," *Bernama*, January 24, 2008.
[25] "US to Sign FTA with Other Countries if Talks with Malaysia Fail," *Bernama*, January 24, 2008.
[26] Ibid.
[27] "US Aims to Conclude FTA by Summer, Insists on Government Procurement," *Bernama*, January 17, 2008.
[28] "No Need for Deadline to Conclude Malaysia-US FTA, Says Rafidah," *Bernama*, January 24, 2008.
[29] For more information on Malaysia's general elections of 2008, see CRS Report RL33878, *U.S.-Malaysia Relations: Implications of the 2008 Elections*, by Michael F. Martin.
[30] Mohd Arshi Mat daud, "9th Round of Malaysia-US FTA Talks in November, Says Muhyiddin," *Bernama*, July 24, 2008.
[31] "Free Trade Pact with US: No Compromise in Sensitive Areas," *The Malaysian Insider*, May 26, 2008.
[32] Rupa Damodaran, "Some Compromise in Malaysia-U.S. Trade Talks?," *Business Times*, July 22, 2008.
[33] Ibid.
[34] "KL to Discuss Procurement in US FTA Talks," *Malaysian Insider*, October 1, 2008.

[35] For more information in the U.S. FTA with Singapore, see CRS Report RL34315, *The U.S.-Singapore Free Trade Agreement: Effects After Three Years*, by Dick K. Nanto
[36] "US Adopts Pragmatic Approach in FTA Talks: MIER," *Bernama*, July 22, 2008.
[37] Mohd Arshi Mat Daud, "9th Round of Malaysia-US FTA Talks in November," *Bernama*, July 24, 2008.
[38] Hamidah Atan, "PM Hopes to See Fairer Trade Ties with US," *New Strait TImes*, November 7, 2008.
[39] "US Wants to Hold Back FTA Talks with Malaysia for a While," *Bernama*, November 26, 2008.
[40] "US Keen to Conclude FTA with Malaysia," *Bernama*, December 15, 2008.
[41] "PM Condemns 'Disproportionate' Israeli Military Action," *Malaysiakini*, December 29, 2008.
[42] "Malaysia Condemns Israel's Air Strikes in Gaza," *Bernama*, December 29, 2008.
[43] "Gaza Prompts Boycott in Malaysia," *BBC News*, January 9, 2009.
[44] "Review FTA Negotiations with United States," *Bernama*, January 10, 2009.
[45] "Rundingan FTA Dengan AS Dihentikan Sementara," *Utasan (in Malay)*, January 12, 2009; translation provided by U.S. Embassy in Kuala Lumpur.
[46] "PM to Muhyiddin: Explain Statement on Suspension of FTA Talks with US," *The Malaysian Insider*, January 13, 2009.
[47] "US Postponed US-Malayia FTA Talks," *Bernama*, January 15, 2009.
[48] Business Software Alliance, *Fifth Annual BSA and IDC Global Software Piracy Study*, Washington, D.C., June 19, 2008.
[49] Office of the U. S. Trade Representative, *2008 Special 301 Report*, Washington, D.C., April 25, 2008, p. 42,
http://www.ustr.gov/assets 553_14869.pdf.
[50] Ibid.
[51] TRIPs refers to the 1995 Agreement on Trade-Related Aspects of Intellectual Property Rights. For more information on TRIPs, TRIPs plus, and FTAs, see CRS Report RL34292, *Intellectual Property Rights and International Trade*, by Shayerah Ilias and Ian F. Fergusson.
[52] For more on the CL provisions of TRIPs, see CRS Report RL33750, *The WTO, Intellectual Property Rights, and the Access to Medicines Controversy*, by Ian F. Fergusson.
[53] For an explanation of data exclusivity and its inclusion in FTAs, see CRS Report RL33288, *Proprietary Rights in Pharmaceutical Innovation: Issues at the Intersection of Patents and Marketing Exclusivities*, by John R. Thomas.
[54] Soon Li Tsin, "People with HIV/AIDS Hold Anti-FTA Protest," *Malaysiakini*, January 11, 2007.
[55] Dass, Maria J. Groups Worried Over FTA with US. *Sun2Surf*, September 11, 2006.
[56] U.S. Trade Representative. *2007 National Trade Estimate Report on Foreign Trade Barriers*, April 7, 2007. Section on Malaysia.
[57] A copy of the ATPC's testimony is available online at http://www.us-asean.org/US-Malaysia Automotive_Trade_Policy_Council.pdf
[58] For more information on foreign objections to U.S. SPS regulations, see CRS Report RL33472, *Sanitary and Phytosanitary (SPS) Concerns in Agricultural Trade*, by Geoffrey S. Becker.
[59] U.S. to Face Difficulties on Financial Services in Malaysia FTA Talks, *Inside U.S. Trade*, March 10, 2006.
[60] U.S. Trade Representative. *2007 National Trade Estimate Report on Foreign Trade Barriers*, March 31, 2007. Section on Malaysia.

[61] Ibid.
[62] Ibid.
[63] The negative list of sectors closed to foreign investment, for example, may include airports, social insurance, or other sectors that are run by governments or have special security requirements.
[64] Ibid.
[65] Government Procurement Emerging as Major Problem in U.S.-Malaysia FTA. *Inside US Trade*, September 1, 2006.
[66] Malaysia's computer manufacturers – including facilities owned by U.S. companies – are apparently particularly interested in access to the U.S. government procurement market.
[67] Rupa Damodaran, "Manufacturers: US FTA Talks Could be Faster," *New Strait Times*, December 17, 2007.
[68] Kevin Tan, "Procurement Left Out in FTA Talks," *The Edge Daily*, January 18, 2008.
[69] Office of Senator Max Baucus. *Baucus Welcomes Launch of U.S.-Malaysia Free Trade Talks*, Press Release, March 2006. Office of Congressman Jim Kolbe. *Kolbe Hails Free Trade Negotiations with Malaysia*, Press Release, March 2006. Office of Congressman Dan Burton. *Vice-Chairman Burton Comments on the Launch of the United States-Malaysia Free Trade Agreement*, March 7, 2006.
[70] National Association of Manufacturers. Testimony of Christopher Wenk before the Trade Policy Staff Committee, Office of the U.S. Trade Representative, on "Proposed United States-Malaysia Free Trade Agreement," May 3, 2006.
[71] The web page for the U.S.-Malaysia Free Trade Agreement (FTA) Business Coalition is http://www.us-asean.org/ US-Malaysia%20FTA/index.asp. The Secretariat for the US-Malaysia Free Trade Agreement Business Coalition is the US-ASEAN Business Council.
[72] The website, "FTA Malaysia," http://www.ftamalaysia.org/ is a nexus for information provided by groups, organizations and individuals opposed to the U.S.-Malaysia FTA.
[73] For more information on U.S.-Malaysia relations, see CRS Report RL33878, *U.S.-Malaysia Relations: Implications of the 2008 Elections*, by Michael F. Martin.
[74] The White House. National Security Strategy of the United States. March 2006, part VI.
[75] See CRS Report RL31038, *Asia Pacific Economic Cooperation (APEC) and the 2007 Meetings in Sydney, Australia*, by Michael F. Martin.
[76] Office of the United States Trade Representative. Free Trade Agreement: U.S.-Malaysia. Trade Facts, March 2006.
[77] Remarks by Ambassador Karan K. Bhatia, Deputy U.S. Trade Representative, Press Conference on the U.S.- Malaysia Free Trade Agreement, Kuala Lumpur, Malaysia, March 17, 2006.
[78] Malaysia. Ministry of Trade and Industry. Malaysia-US Free Trade Agreement. Media Release. May 3, 2006.
[79] Malaysia. Ministry of Trade and Industry. "Joint Announcement To Launch Negotiations For A Malaysia United States Free Trade Agreement, 8 March 2006, Washington D.C." Media Release, March 13, 2006.
[80] "Chile and Malaysia to Start FTA Talks," *Prensa Latina*, April 19, 2007.
[81] Weisel, Barbara. Opening Remarks, Public Hearing, U.S.-Malaysia FTA, Washington, DC, May 3, 2006.
[82] "Malaysia PM Abdullah Warns Muslims Against Extremism." Voice of America. January 27, 2005. See also CRS Report RL31672, *Terrorism in Southeast Asia*, coordinated by Bruce Vaughn.
[83] Weisel, Barbara. Opening Remarks, May 3, 2006. Op. cit.

[84] The AFL-CIO and the Malaysian Trades Unions Congress signed a joint declaration regarding a U.S.-Malaysia FTA on January 22, 2007, in Kuala Lumpur, stating that any agreement "must result in broadly shared benefits to working people and communities, not simply extend and enforce corporate power and privilege." For more details, see "U.S. Unions Oppose Free Trade with Malaysia," by Anil Netto, Inter Press Service News Agency, January 22, 2007.

[85] AFL-CIO. Issue Brief: The Bush Record on Shipping Jobs Overseas. August 2004. See also: Testimony of Thea M. Lee, Policy Director, American Federation of Labor and Congress of Industrial Organizations (AFL-CIO), before the House of Representatives Committee on Ways and Means, Hearing on the Implementation of the United States-Bahrain Free Trade Agreement, September 29, 2005.

[86] See, for example, Testimony of Thea M. Lee, Policy Director, AFL-CIO, before the Subcommittee on International Trade of the Senate Committee on Finance in a Hearing on the Implementation of the United States-Oman Free Trade Agreement, March 6, 2006.

[87] U.S. Department of State. Bureau of Democracy, Human Rights, and Labor. *Country Reports on Human Rights Practices—2007, Malaysia.* March 11, 2008.

[88] For more information on the condition of immigrant workers in Malaysia, see Human Rights Watch report on Malaysia at http://hrw.org/doc/?t=asia&c=malays.

[89] "20,000 Fishermen, Farmers Protest Against FTA," by Fauwaz Abdul Aziz, Malaysiakini, January 10, 2007.

[90] "Malaysians Concerned Over Possible Free Trade Agreement with US," by Joseph Masiliamany, AsiaNews, October 10, 2006.

[91] Public Citizen. Global Trade Watch. CAFTA: Part of the FTAA Puzzle. http://www.citizen.org/trade

[92] "People with HIV/AIDS Hold Anti-FTA Protest," by Soon Li Tsin, Malaysiakini, January 11, 2007; "US FTA: Will We Lose Out, Too?" by Jacqueline Ann Surin, *The Sun*, January 11, 2007.

[93] See CRS Report RL33961, *Arab League Boycott of Israel*, by Martin A. Weiss.

[94] See CRS Report RL31870, *The Dominican Republic-Central America-United States Free Trade Agreement (CAFTA-DR)*, by J. F. Hornbeck.

[95] For a more general discussion of the potential trade effects of FTAs, see CRS Report RL31356, *Free Trade Agreements: Impact on U.S. Trade and Implications for U.S. Trade Policy*, by William H. Cooper.

[96] Office of the U.S. Trade Representative. "United States and Malaysia Sign Trade and Investment Framework Agreement." Press Release. May 10, 2004.

[97] See World Trade Organization discussion of the Information Technology Agreement at http://www.wto.org/English/ tratop_e/inftec_e/inftec_e.htm.

[98] Wenk, Christopher. Testimony on the Proposed United States-Malaysia Free Trade Agreement For the Trade Policy Staff Committee, Office of the U.S. Trade Representative. May 3, 2006.

[99] Purchasing power parity estimates of per capita GDP attempt to revalue official GDP figures by comparing the relative costs of a select group of goods in each nation and then recalculating per capita GDP to reflect the relative purchasing power in each nation.

[100] Source: Malaysia Industrial Development Authority http://www.mida.gov.my/. Figure includes approved projects.

[101] For more detailed information about trade promotion authority, see CRS Report RL33743, *Trade Promotion Authority (TPA): Issues, Options, and Prospects for Renewal*, by J. F. Hornbeck and William H. Cooper.

[102] This chronology is based on various news reports, press releases, and notifications.
[103] Malaysia does not qualify for GSP treatment.
[104] Based on the most current World Trade Organization Trade Policy Reviews for Malaysia and the United States.
[105] Office of the United States Trade Representative. "Free Trade Agreement: U.S. and Malaysia, Economic and Strategic Benefits." Power Point presentation. March 8, 2006. http://www.ustr.gov/assets Fact_Sheets/2006/asset_upload_file802_9121.pdf

In: Malaysia: Country Profile and U.S. Relations   ISBN: 978-1-61470-172-9
Editors: G. A. Villalobos, D. E. Segura © 2011 Nova Science Publishers, Inc.

Chapter 4

MALAYSIA: COUNTRY ANALYSIS BRIEFS[*]

Energy Information Administration

BACKGROUND

Although Malaysia's oil fields are maturing, new offshore developments of both oil and gas are expected to increase aggregate production capacity in the near- to mid-term. Malaysia's western coast runs alongside the Strait of Malacca, an important route for seaborne energy trade that links the Indian and Pacific Oceans.

> Malaysia is a significant net exporter of oil and the second largest exporter of liquefied natural gas (LNG) in the world behind Qatar

OIL

According to the Oil & Gas Journal (OGJ), Malaysia held proven oil reserves of 4 billion barrels as of January 2009. Nearly all of Malaysia's oil comes from offshore fields. The continental shelf is divided into 3 producing basins: the Malay basin in the west and the Sarawak and Sabah basins in the east. Most of the country's oil reserves are located in the Malay basin and tend

---

[*] This is an edited, reformatted and augmented version of a Energy Information Administration publication, from www.eia.doe.gov, dated September 2009.

to be of high quality. Malaysia's benchmark crude oil, Tapis Blend, is very light and sweet with an API gravity of 44° and sulfur content of 0.08 percent by weight. More than half of total Malaysian oil production comes from the Tapis field.

Malaysia's oil reserves are the third highest in the Asia-Pacific region

Source: Oil and Gas Journal.

Sector Organization

Malaysia's national oil company, Petroleam Nasional Berhad (Petronas), dominates upstream and downstream activities in the country's oil sector. Petronas is the only remaining wholly state-owned enterprise in Malaysia and is the single largest contributor of government revenues. Petronas holds exclusive ownership rights to all exploration and production projects in Malaysia, and all foreign and private companies must operate through production sharing contracts (PSCs) with Petronas. ExxonMobil (through its local subsidiary Esso Production Malaysia Inc.) is the largest foreign oil company by production volume, and there are numerous other foreign companies operating in Malaysia via PSCs, including Shell, Chevron, and BP.

All energy policy in Malaysia is crafted and overseen by the Economic Planning Unit (EPU) and the Implementation and Coordination Unit (ICU), which report directly to the Prime Minister. The Ministry of Energy, Water, and Communications regulates the hydrocarbon and electricity sectors, although it does not have policymaking powers.

Exploration and Production

Total oil production in 2008 was 727,000 barrels per day (bbl/d). During 2008, Malaysia consumed an estimated 547,000 bbl/d, and had net exports of about 180,000 bbl/d. Petronas and its various PSC partners are most active exploring offshore areas. Since 2002, the focus has been on deepwater fields on the eastern continental shelf that pose high operating costs and require substantial technical expertise. Petronas announced in January 2009 that 7 new oil fields had come online in 2008, making for a total of 68 producing oil fields.

New oil production projects in the planning or construction phase include:

The Gumusat/Kakap project, located offshore Sabah in 3,937 feet of deep water, will include the regions' first deepwater floating production system with processing capacity of 150,000 bbl/d. from 19 subsea wells. The system will be connected via pipelines to a new oil and gas terminal to be built in Kimanis, Sabah. In March 2009, it was reported that the engineering contract was awarded and that the offshore installation will begin in 2010. Shell is the operator, holding 33 percent interest; ConocoPhillips also holds 33 percent interest, Petronas has 20 percent and Murphy Oil has 14 percent.

Malaysia's Oil Production and Consumption, 1988-2008

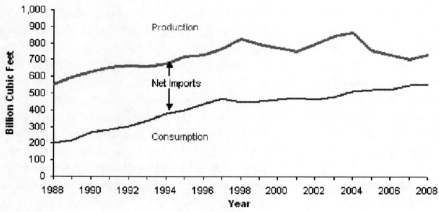

Source: EIA.

Shell is also the operator at the Malikai oil field with 35 percent interest, in partnership with ConocoPhillips at 35 percent and Petronas with 30 percent. The field was discovered in 2004 at 1,854 feet subsea offshore Sabah. In August 2009 Shell invited bids for engineering and design services. Malakai is expected to come online in 2012 with production of up to 150,000 bbl/d.

In March 2009, the North Fields development, located offshore Malaysia near Vietnam, reportedly began producing oil. The North Field is expected to produce between 40,000 and 50,000 bbl/d by early 2010. Talisman Energy (Canada), the operator, has plans to drill 16 development wells in 2009 and another 13 in 2010.

Brunei and Malaysia signed an agreement in March 2009 to settle their maritime territorial dispute that has prevented exploration of the rich offshore oil reserves off Borneo for the past 6 years. Both countries are expected to cooperate on the development of the sites but no timeframe was given.

Downstream Activities

According to OGJ, Malaysia had about 515,000 bbl/d of refining capacity at six facilities as of January 2009. Petronas operates three refineries (259,000 bbl/d total capacity), while Shell operates two plants (170,000 bbl/d total capacity), and ExxonMobil operates one (86,000 bbl/d). Malaysia invested heavily in refining activities during the last two decades, and is now able to meet most of the country's demand for petroleum products domestically, after relying on the refining industry in Singapore for many years.

NATURAL GAS

According to OGJ, Malaysia held 83 trillion cubic feet (Tcf) of proven natural gas reserves as of January 2009. While much of the country's oil reserves are found off Peninsular Malaysia, much of the country's natural gas production comes from Eastern Malaysia, offshore Sarawak and Sabah.

> Malaysia is the world's eighth largest holder of natural gas reserves and was the second largest exporter of liquefied natural gas after Qatar in 2007

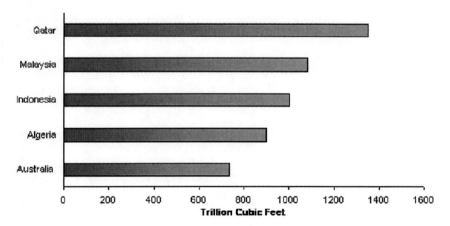

Source: EIA.

Sector Organization

As in the oil sector, Malaysia's state-owned Petronas dominates the natural gas sector. The company has a monopoly on all upstream natural gas developments, and also plays a leading role in downstream activities and LNG trade. Most natural gas production occurs from PSCs operated by foreign companies in conjunction with Petronas.

Exploration and Production

Natural gas production has been rising steadily, reaching 2.3 Tcf in 2007, while domestic natural gas consumption has also increased steadily, reaching 1.2 Tcf in 2007. There are several important ongoing projects that are expected to expand natural gas production in Malaysia over the near term. E&P activities in Malaysia continue to focus on offshore areas, especially deepwater blocks.

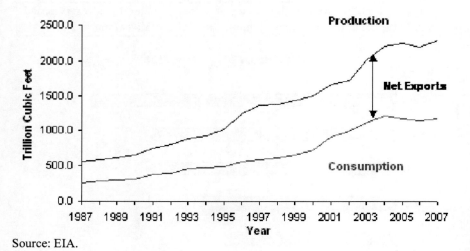

Source: EIA.

Malaysia-Thailand Joint Development Area

One of the most active areas for natural gas exploration and production is the Malaysia-Thailand Joint Development Area (JDA), located in the lower part of the Gulf of Thailand. The area is divided into three blocks, Block A-18, Block B-17, and Block C-19, and is administered by the Malaysia-Thailand Joint Authority (MTJA), with each country owning 50 percent of the JDA's hydrocarbon resources (map of the JDA). The JDA reportedly holds 9.5 Tcf of proved plus probable natural gas reserves. The Carigali-Triton Operating Company (CTOC), a joint venture between Petronas Carigali and Hess, operates Block A-18, while Blocks B-17 and C-19 are operated by the Carigali-PTTEP Operating Company (CPOC), a joint venture of each country's national oil company.

Pipelines

Malaysia has one of the most extensi ve natural gas pipeline networks in Asia. The Peninsular Gas Utilization (PGU) project, completed in 1998, expanded the natural gas transmission infrastructure on Peninsular Malaysia. The PGU system spans more than 880 miles and has the capacity to transport 2 billion cubic feet per day (Bcf/d) of natural gas. Pipelines now connect Malaysia with Singapore and Indonesia, and the Trans-Thailand-Malaysia Gas Pipeline System allows Malaysia to pipe natural gas from the Malaysia-Thailand JDA to its domestic pipeline system. This linkage marks a significant step toward the realization of the proposed "Trans-ASEAN Gas Pipeline" (TAGP) system, a transnational pipeline network linking the major natural gas producers and consumers in Southeast Asia. Because of Malaysia's extensi ve natural gas infrastructure and its location, the country is a natural candidate to serve as a hub in the proposed TAGP project.

Petronas is also reportedly planning to build the 310-mile Sabah-Sarawak Gas Pipeline between Kimanis, Sabah and Bintulu, Sarawak to transport gas from Sabah's offshore fields, such as Kota Kinabalu, to Bintulu for liquefaction and export. Some of the gas will be used for downstream projects in Sabah. The pipeline is expected to be completed by March 2011. Howe ver, while en vironmental approval has been recei ved, land acquisition issues are still being finalized.

Exports

Malaysia was the second largest exporter of LNG in the world after Qatar in 2007, exporting over 1 Tcf of LNG, which accounted for 13 percent of total world LNG exports. Japan, South Korea, and Taiwan were the 3 primary purchasers. LNG is primarily transported by Malaysia International Shipping Corporation (MISC), which owns and operates 27 LNG tankers, the single largest LNG tanker fleet in the world by volume of LNG carried. MISC is 62-percent owned by Petronas and also has significant in vol vement in oil shipping acti vities.

Petronas owns majority interests in Malaysia's 3 LNG processing plants, all located in a complex at Bintulu, Sarawak (East Malaysia) and supplied by the offshore natural gas fields at Sarawak. The Bintulu facility is the largest LNG complex in the world, with 8 production trains and a total liquefaction capacity of 1.1 Tcf per year. A further increment through debottlenecking is expected by 2010, raising overall capacity by 0.6 Tcf per year. As the main LNG importer in Asia, Japanese financing has been critical to the development of Malaysia's LNG facilities.

Construction began on the Sabah Oil and Gas Terminal (SOGT) in February 2007 and is expected to be completed by January 2010. It will have handling capacity of 300,000 barrels of crude and 1 billion cubic feet of natural gas per day and will primarily serve export markets. The Sabah-Sarawak Gas Pipeline project is part of this development.

PROFILE

Energy Overview

Proven Oil Reserves (January 1, 2009E)	4 billion barrels
Oil Production (2008E)	727,000 bbl/d, of which 84% was crude oil
Oil Consumption (2008E)	547,000 bbl/d
Crude Oil Distillation Capacity (January 1, 2009E)	514,832 bbl/d
Proven Natural Gas Reserves (January 1, 2009E)	83 trillion cubic feet
Natural Gas Production (2007E)	2.3 trillion cubic feet
Natural Gas Consumption (2007E)	1.2 trillion cubic feet
Recoverable Coal Reserves (2008E)	4.4 million short tons
Coal Production (2007E)	1.1 million short tons
Coal Consumption (2007E)	18.5 million short tons
Electricity Installed Capacity (2006E)	23.3 gigawatts
Electricity Production (2006E)	99.1 billion kilowatt hours
Electricity Consumption (2006E)	96.0 billion kilowatt hours
Total Energy Consumption (2006E)	2.56 quadrillion Btu*, of which Natural Gas (35%), Oil (41%), Coal (15%), Hydroelectricity (2%)
Total Per Capita Energy Consumption ((Million Btu) (2006E)	99.4 million Btu per person
Energy Intensity (2006E)	8,891 Btu per $2000-PPP**

Environmental Overview

Energy-Related Carbon Dioxide Emissions (2006E)	163.5 million Metric tons, of which Oil (44%), Natural Gas (41%), Coal (15%)
Per-Capita, Energy-Related Carbon Dioxide Emissions ((Metric Tons of Carbon Dioxide) (2006E)	6.7 Metric tons
Carbon Dioxide Intensity (2006E)	0.6 Metric tons per thousand $2000-PPP**

Oil and Gas Industry

Organization	Malaysia's state-owned Petroleam Nasional Berhad (Petronas) dominates all aspects of the country's oil and natural gas sector.
Major Oil/Gas Ports	Kertih, Johor, Sepangar Bay, Bintulu, Kuching, Melaka, Penang, Port Dickson, Kelang, Kota Kinabalu, Kemaman
Foreign Company Involvement	BP, ConocoPhillips, ExxonMobil (Esso), Hess, Mitsubishi, Murphy Oil, Newfield Exploration, Nippon Oil, Shell, Talisman Energy
Major Oil Fields	Bekok, Bokor, Erb West, Bunga Kekwa, Guntong, Kepong, Kinabalu, Samarang, Seligi, Semangkok, Tapis, Temana, Tiong
Major Natural Gas Fields	Bedong, Bintang, Damar, Jerneh, Laho, Lawit, Noring, Pilong, Resak, Telok, Tujoh
Major Refineries (capacity, bbl/d)(January 1, 2009)	Shell: Port Dickson (125,000), Lutong (45,000); Petronas: Melaka I (92,832), Melaka II (126,000), Kertih (40,000); EssoMalaysia: Port Dickson (86,000)

* The total energy consumption statistic includes petroleum, dry natural gas, coal, net hydro, nuclear, geothermal, solar, wind, wood and waste electric power.
**GDP figures from Global Insight estimates based on purchasing power parity (PPP) exchange rates.

Links

EIA Links
EIA – Malaysia Country Energy Profile
U.S. Government
CIA World Factbook - Malaysia

U.S. State Department Consular Information Sheet - Malaysia
U.S. Embassy in Malaysia
Foreign Government Agencies
Department of Statistics Malaysia
Malaysia-Thailand Joint Authority
Ministry of Energy, Water, and Communications, Malaysia
BP Statistical Review
ExxonMobil Malaysia
Murphy Oil in Malaysia
Petroleam Nasional Berhad (Petronas)
Shell in Malaysia

Sources

Asian Energy
Associated Press
Association of Southeast Asian Nations (ASEAN)
CDiver
CEDIGAZ
Daily Express (Eastern Malaysia)
Dow Jones Newswires
Dow Jones Commodities service
Economist Intelligence Unit
Energy Files
Esso Production Malaysia Inc. (EPMI)
Global Insight
Hess Corporation
International Oil Daily
Jonesday
Malaysia-Thailand Joint Authority
Murphy Oil
Natural Gas Week
NewsBase Asia Oil and Gas Monitor
Oil & Gas Journal
Oil Week
Petroleum Economist
Petroleum Intelligence Weekly
Petronas

Platts Oilgram News
Reuters
Rigzone
Shell
SubseaIQ
The Star (Malaysia)
Upstream
World Gas Intelligence

INDEX

#

9/11, 46

A

abuse, 66
access, 12, 27, 33, 39, 52, 53, 56, 61, 62, 64, 67, 71, 73, 91
accommodation, 17
accounting, 61, 73
adhesives, 68
adverse effects, 66
advocacy, 66
affirmative action, 6
Afghanistan, 38
age, 3
agencies, 29, 66
agricultural exports, 56
agricultural sector, 77
agriculture, 2, 25, 56, 77
AIDS, 59
airports, 91
Alaska, 87
animal husbandry, 25
Anti-Terrorism Assistance (ATA), 43
apparel industry, 67
apparel products, 67
apples, 77
appropriations, 66
architects, 61
Argentina, 26, 59, 68
ASEAN, 9, 20, 21, 22, 23, 29, 35, 36, 40, 46, 47, 48, 54, 60, 63, 64, 65, 71, 91, 101, 104
Asia, vii, 7, 8, 9, 12, 20, 27, 29, 32, 35, 36, 40, 45, 46, 47, 48, 49, 63, 64, 71, 91, 96, 101, 102, 104
Asia Pacific Economic Cooperation, 9, 20, 47, 63, 91
Asia Pacific Economic Cooperation (APEC), 9, 20, 47, 63, 91
Asian values, 7
assessment, 55
assets, 8, 18, 47, 88, 90, 93
Association of Southeast Asian Nations, 9, 35, 104
atrocities, 58
authorities, 42, 80
authority, 5, 18, 92
automobiles, 26, 33, 52, 53, 58, 60, 81
automotive sector, 60
awareness, 10

B

Bahrain, 92
banks, 8, 61
Barisan Nasional (BN), vii, 6, 11, 13, 56
barriers, 33, 34, 52, 60, 67, 68, 69, 76

base, 15
Bawadi Administration, 35
benefits, 26, 52, 63, 92
beverages, 3
bilateral relationship, 11, 23, 37, 39
bilateral ties, 37
biotechnology, 34
blame, 23
Buddhism, 2
Burma, 21, 36, 39, 46, 47
business environment, 9
businesses, 8, 33, 58, 63
buyer, 31

C

Cabinet, 18, 44, 53, 57, 58, 62, 75
Cambodia, 46, 47
candidates, 15
capacity building, 40, 42, 67
capital goods, 26
capitalism, 7
Capitol Hill, 32
category a, 77
central bank, 8, 24, 29, 61
challenges, 22
chemical, 73, 74
chemical industry, 74
chemicals, 3
children, 22
Chile, 64, 68, 91
China, 1, 3, 21, 22, 27, 28, 29, 35, 36, 41, 42, 46, 55, 63, 64, 70, 71
Christianity, 2
Christians, 3
CIA, 103
cities, 1
citizenship, 6, 17
City, 6
civil law, 5
civilization, 20
classification, 80
cleavages, 16
clothing, 64, 79, 81
coal, 103

Coast Guard, 41
cocoa, 3, 78
collaboration, 56, 64
Colombia, 56, 65, 69
color, iv
commerce, 6
commercial, 4, 11, 22, 61, 65
commercial bank, 61
commodity, 22, 77
commodity markets, 22
common law, 5
communication, 8, 41
Communist Party, 17
communities, 92
community, 15, 17, 30, 36, 62
competition, 22, 53, 56, 60, 67
competition policy, 53, 56, 67
competitiveness, 63, 64
composition, 16
computer, 73, 91
conference, 40
conflict, 12, 21, 23, 38
confrontation, 4
Congress, iv, viii, 11, 15, 18, 32, 34, 45, 47, 51, 52, 63, 74, 75, 76, 92
consensus, 21
Constitution, 2
construction, 2, 42, 97
consumers, 67, 101
consumption, 24, 100, 103
controversial, 51, 53, 63
convention, 89
conviction, 7
cooperation, vii, 9, 11, 12, 22, 23, 37, 39, 40, 41, 42, 64, 65
copyright, iv
Copyright, iv
corruption, 7
cost, 59, 66
counterterrorism, vii, 10, 11, 37, 39, 40, 41, 65
Court of Appeals, 3
covering, 64
CPI, 25, 68
crawling peg, 46

Index

criticism, 39, 65
crop, 25, 60
crops, 25, 53
crude oil, 96, 102
culture, 20, 89
currency, 9, 22, 61

D

Darfur, 43, 49
deaths, 42
deficit, 27
Delta, 21
democracy, 2, 18, 36
Department of Labor, 76
deployments, 9
deprivation, 38
deregulation, 66
diplomacy, 23
direct investment, 9
disaster, 41
disaster relief, 41
discrimination, 42
District of Columbia, 87
Doha, 35, 37, 47, 63
domestic demand, 24
Dominican Republic, 66, 92
draft, 74, 76
drugs, 41, 59, 66

E

earnings, 26
East Asia, 12, 21, 29, 35, 45, 47
East Timor, 20, 35
economic activity, 67
economic cooperation, 23
economic development, 7, 13, 64
economic downturn, 24, 46
economic growth, 9, 12, 18, 19, 24, 27, 28, 63, 64
economic indicator, 68
economic integration, 12
economic policy, 8, 23

economic progress, 7
economic reform, 16
economic reforms, 16
economic relations, 63
economic transformation, 64
economics, vii, 11
education, 7, 29, 65
educational system, 29
election, vii, 7, 11, 13, 14, 15, 16, 19, 44
electrical and electronics (E&E), 26
electricity, 97
embassy, 6, 55
employers, 66
employment, 26, 76
encouragement, 57
energy, viii, 22, 33, 95, 97
enforcement, 33, 41, 52, 58, 59, 65, 67
engineering, 97, 98
environment, 8, 56
environmental issues, 54
environmental protection, 65
environmental standards, 65, 66
epidemic, 59
equipment, 3, 26, 31, 40, 41, 44, 73, 74, 77, 79, 81
equity, 61
ethnic Chinese, vii, 3, 6, 16, 17, 29, 88
ethnic groups, 3, 17, 18, 29, 88
ethnicity, 14, 17
European Union, 23, 35, 36
evidence, 14, 27, 29, 54
exchange rate, 24, 29, 46, 68, 103
exchange rate policy, 29
exercise, 41
expertise, 97
exploitation, 22, 66
Export Control and Related Border Security Assistance (EXBS), 43
export market, 12, 27, 52, 70, 71, 73, 102
exporter, 76, 95, 99, 101
exporters, 8, 52, 58, 64, 67, 71, 77
exports, 3, 12, 24, 26, 27, 29, 30, 31, 33, 42, 53, 64, 67, 68, 69, 81, 101
exposure, 8, 40
extremists, 19

F

faith, 5
farmers, 25, 60, 63, 65, 66
FAS, 82
FDI, 29, 30, 31, 33, 46, 64, 68
federal government, 5, 16
Federal Government, 18
feelings, 55
financial, 7, 8, 9, 10, 24, 26, 33, 52, 53, 56, 61, 71
financial crisis, 7, 8, 26, 53, 61
financial development, 9
financial markets, 24, 27, 53
financial sector, 61
fires, 23
fiscal deficit, 28, 29
fish, 3, 81
fisheries, 79
fishing, 25, 66
flexibility, 9, 64
flour, 77
flowers, 78
food, 3, 15, 77, 80
footwear, 79, 81
force, 2, 24, 29, 38, 57, 71
foreign affairs, 24
foreign assistance, 43
foreign banks, 61
foreign companies, 27, 61, 97, 99
foreign direct investment, 9, 29, 30, 31, 64
foreign exchange, 8
foreign investment, 69, 91
foreign policy, 9, 65
forest fire, 23
formation, 4, 15, 29, 35
France, 42, 45, 46, 49
free trade, vii, viii, 9, 12, 16, 30, 32, 33, 34, 35, 36, 51, 52, 53, 55, 63, 64, 65, 67, 68, 75, 76
free trade agreement (FTA), viii, 12, 16, 32, 51, 52, 53
free trade area, 35, 36, 64
freedom, 42, 57
friction, 23

full employment, 28
funding, 43, 67

G

GDP, 3, 8, 9, 24, 25, 26, 29, 68, 92, 103
general election, 7, 13, 20, 56, 89
Generalized System of Preferences, 77
Georgia, 87
Germany, 27, 28, 32
global demand, 26
globalization, 12, 51, 63, 65
goods and services, 12, 29, 55, 58, 64, 76
government procurement, 33, 52, 53, 56, 58, 62, 91
government revenues, 97
governments, viii, 7, 11, 15, 16, 19, 38, 91
grants, 16
gravity, 96
Greece, 26, 59
gross domestic product, 8, 24
growth, 3, 8, 9, 24, 29, 30, 77
growth rate, 3
guidance, 58

H

Hamas, 89
harmony, 6, 7, 18
Hawaii, 45, 87
health, 23, 27, 59
history, 7, 10, 17, 57
HIV, 59, 66, 90, 92
HIV/AIDS, 59, 66, 90, 92
Hong Kong, 22, 28, 31
House, 2, 5, 33, 41, 47, 54, 92
House of Representatives, 2, 5, 47, 92
hub, 101
human, 22, 36, 40, 42, 46
human right, 36, 40, 42
human rights, 36, 40, 42

Index

I

ideals, 40
ideology, 20
IMF, 7
imports, 3, 12, 24, 26, 27, 29, 31, 42, 52, 53, 60, 69, 70, 71, 77, 81
improvements, 59
impulses, 37
inauguration, 51, 52, 54, 58
income, 8, 9, 12, 14, 15, 24, 29, 68
increased competition, 69
independence, vii, 4, 5, 6, 11, 13, 15, 17, 23
Independence, 2
India, 28, 35, 36, 42, 47, 64, 71, 89
Indians, 16, 17
indigenous peoples, 5, 8
individuals, 91
Indonesia, 4, 9, 20, 21, 22, 23, 24, 25, 28, 39, 40, 42, 46, 47, 49, 64, 65, 66, 101
industrial sectors, 81
industries, 51, 63, 64, 67, 69
industry, 2, 6, 26, 32, 42, 52, 59, 60, 66, 74, 77, 99
inequality, 29
inflation, 14, 15, 29, 68
information technology, 67
infrastructure, 7, 101
insurgency, 5
integrated circuits, 31
intellectual property, 12, 33, 52, 53, 55, 58, 59, 67
intellectual property rights, 12, 33, 52, 53, 55, 58
intelligence, 17, 42
interest groups, 53, 66, 74
International Military Education and Training (IMET), 41, 43, 44
International Monetary Fund, 7
International Narcotics Control, 43, 44
international terrorism, 38
international trade, vii, 12, 32, 36
International Visitor Leadership Program (IVLP), 10
interoperability, 44

investment, vii, 9, 10, 12, 24, 29, 32, 34, 35, 36, 37, 42, 55, 56, 61, 64, 67, 69, 73
investment bank, 61
investments, 24, 73
investors, 42, 67, 74
Iowa, 87
IPR, 33, 53, 56, 58, 59
Iran, 26, 32, 33, 37, 38, 47, 59
Iraq, 12, 37, 38, 39, 45
Islam, 2, 3, 4, 7, 14, 18, 19, 20, 29, 38, 39, 45, 48, 65
Islamic state, 20, 39
Israel, 38, 52, 53, 57, 58, 66, 89, 90, 92
issues, viii, 12, 15, 21, 22, 23, 32, 33, 37, 51, 52, 53, 55, 57, 58, 59, 67, 75, 76, 101

J

Japan, 3, 27, 28, 29, 31, 35, 64, 70, 71, 101
Java, 4
Jews, 36
job creation, 64
Jordan, 74
judiciary, 18
jumping, 14
jurisdiction, 5

K

Korea, 35
Kosovo, 9
Kuala Lumpur, vii, 1, 2, 6, 10, 13, 16, 21, 33, 39, 45, 55, 57, 64, 75, 89, 90, 91, 92
Kuwait, 42

L

labor force, 65
labor market, 76
labor markets, 76
land acquisition, 101
Laos, 21, 46, 47
laws, 59, 65, 75
lawyers, 61

lead, 21, 38, 61, 74
leadership, 19, 20, 21
Lebanon, 9, 38
legal issues, 55
legislation, 66, 74
liberalization, vii, 12, 29, 32, 34, 35, 64
light, 96
liquefied natural gas, 3, 33, 95, 99
living conditions, 23
logging, 23
Louisiana, 87

M

machinery, 3, 30, 31, 77, 79, 81
macroeconomic policies, 29
majority, 3, 5, 7, 14, 17, 23, 67, 102
management, 8, 44
manufacturing, 2, 8, 9, 25, 26, 32, 60, 73
marginalization, 37
market access, 12, 33, 35, 53, 56, 58, 62, 64
Maryland, 87
matter, iv, 58
Mauritius, 26, 60
media, 43, 53
membership, 4, 15
merchandise, 27, 69, 73
Mexico, 1, 13, 24, 40, 68, 87
military, 4, 12, 21, 38, 40, 41, 44, 52, 53, 57, 58, 66, 89
military exercises, 41
military-to-military, 44
Ministry of International Trade and Industry (MITI), 58
minorities, 15
missions, 9
Missouri, 87
models, 21
monopoly, 99
Montana, 87
mortality, 2
mortality rate, 2
most favored nation (MFN), 76
multinational corporations, 30
Muslims, 3, 5, 37, 38, 45, 47, 65, 91

Mutual Legal Assistance Treaty (MLAT), 10
Myanmar, 36, 46, 47

N

NAFTA, 65, 66
narcotics, 65
National Association of Manufacturers, 63, 91
natural gas, 3, 99, 100, 101, 102, 103
negotiating, vii, 12, 32, 64, 67, 71, 76
Nepal, 9
net exports, 97
Netherlands, 27, 28
New Zealand, 21, 35, 47, 64, 71
NGOs, 88
Non-Aligned Movement (NAM),, 9, 20
Non-Proliferation Anti-Terrorist Demining and Related Programs (NADR), 43, 44
North America, 65
North American Free Trade Agreement, 65

O

Obama, 51, 52, 54, 57, 65
Obama Administration, 54, 57
Office of the United States Trade Representative, 88, 91, 93
officials, 39, 53, 66
oil, viii, 3, 8, 9, 21, 23, 25, 41, 42, 78, 95, 96, 97, 98, 99, 101, 103
oil production, 96, 97
Oklahoma, 88
open markets, 67, 68
operating costs, 97
operations, 30, 45, 52, 53, 58, 61, 66, 73, 89
opportunities, 24, 63
opposition parties, vii, 7, 10, 11, 13, 14, 66
oppression, 57
opt out, 36
Organization of the Islamic Conference (OIC), 9, 43
outsourcing, 30

P

oversight, 74
ownership, 8, 61, 97

Pacific, viii, 9, 27, 29, 32, 35, 41, 45, 46, 47, 48, 49, 63, 95, 96
Pakistan, 9, 64, 71
palm oil, 25
parity, 25, 92
Parliament, 18, 19
patents, 59
Patriot Act, 39
peace, 5, 9, 20, 23
peace accord, 5
peacekeepers, 43
peacekeeping, 9, 20
Pentagon, 46
per capita income, 3, 24, 46, 68
permission, iv
permit, 43
Peru, 69
petroleum, 3, 42, 77, 99, 103
Petroleum, 3, 79, 104
pharmaceutical, 58, 59, 66
pharmaceuticals, 59
Philippines, 9, 21, 25, 36, 39, 46, 47, 64
piracy, 41
plants, 33, 78, 98, 102
playing, 20
PM, 44, 49, 89, 90, 91
policy, 8, 15, 16, 18, 19, 21, 28, 29, 74, 97
policy options, 74
political leaders, 37
political legitimacy, 19
political parties, 3, 15, 18, 58, 65
political party, vii, 6, 13, 17
political system, 15
politics, 15, 17
pollution, 23
popular vote, 14
population, 2, 3, 8, 16, 18, 22, 39, 88
population growth, 2
poultry, 60
poverty, 23, 29

preferential treatment, 16, 17, 33, 52, 53
prejudice, 37
preparation, iv
president, 15, 37, 62
President, 5, 23, 34, 37, 39, 43, 48, 51, 52, 54, 74, 89
President Obama, 54
presidential campaign, 65
primary products, 8
private investment, 8, 24
privatization, 66
producers, 60, 64, 101
professional development, 10
professionals, 36, 61
project, 24, 42, 61, 97, 101, 102
proliferation, 41
prosperity, 12
protection, 12, 33, 52, 53, 58, 59, 64, 67, 76, 81
public administration, 4
public interest, 58
public investment, 8, 24
public service, 66
Puerto Rico, 88
pulp, 79, 81
purchasing power, 24, 25, 68, 92, 103
purchasing power parity, 24, 25, 68, 103

Q

quotas, 67

R

race, 66
radicalization, 39
raw materials, 26
recession, 24, 46
recognition, 66
recommendations, iv
reelection, 15
reform, 8
reforms, 14, 56
regional cooperation, 21, 35

regionalism, 35
regulations, 58, 60, 67, 90
relative size, 68
relevance, 16
religion, 38
repair, 12
reporters, 43
requirements, 60, 61, 91
reserves, 8, 21, 95, 96, 98, 99, 100
resilience, 8
resources, 3, 22, 24, 100
response, 17, 35, 36, 52, 58
restrictions, 15, 26, 27, 42, 59, 60, 61, 62
rhetoric, 38
rights, iv, 15, 17, 40, 42, 54, 65, 97
risk, 23
risks, 61
root, 16
roots, 21
rubber, 3, 4, 8, 64, 79, 81
rules, 65, 67
rules of origin, 67
rural areas, 25
Russia, 24

S

safety, 12
sanctions, 43
school, 23
security, 5, 10, 17, 22, 24, 42, 91
security forces, 42
semiconductor, 8
semiconductors, 26, 67
Senate, 2, 5, 92
service provider, 56, 63
services, iv, 8, 10, 26, 33, 34, 36, 42, 52, 53, 56, 58, 61, 64, 67, 71, 73, 98
settlements, 4
Sharia, 3
showing, 7, 13, 16, 56
Sierra Leone, 9
signals, 54

Singapore, 2, 3, 4, 17, 21, 23, 26, 28, 31, 35, 36, 39, 40, 41, 42, 46, 47, 49, 60, 64, 65, 67, 70, 71, 90, 99, 101
small businesses, 66
social contract, 6
social justice, 20
society, 3, 10, 16, 37
software, 58
South Asia, 44
South Dakota, 88
South Korea, 25, 27, 28, 29, 35, 55, 56, 57, 64, 65, 67, 101
Southeast Asia, 4, 21, 36, 39, 40, 44, 45, 46, 47, 48, 52, 64, 67, 91, 101
sovereignty, 41
speech, 38
stability, 9, 10, 12, 19, 44
stabilization, 9
state, vii, viii, 1, 2, 4, 5, 6, 7, 8, 10, 11, 14, 15, 16, 17, 18, 19, 21, 23, 24, 36, 40, 42, 47, 63, 66, 97, 99, 103
state enterprises, 9
state legislatures, 5
state of emergency, vii, 5, 6, 17, 23
state-owned enterprises, 8
states, 2, 4, 5, 7, 14, 16, 18, 19, 21, 22, 23, 34, 40, 42
statistics, 27, 30
steel, 8, 83, 86
Strait of Malacca, viii, 12, 24, 41, 63, 65, 95
structure, 18, 25, 30
style, 19
substitution, 69
substitution effect, 69
Sudan, 9, 37, 42, 43, 49
sulfur, 96
Sun, 92
supplier, 27, 31, 52, 70
suppliers, 3, 27, 61
suppression, 12
surplus, 27, 69
sustainable development, 34
sympathy, 36
Syria, 38

Index

T

Taiwan, 22, 27, 28, 71, 101
tariff, 26, 33, 60, 67, 76, 77, 80, 81
tariff rates, 68, 77, 81
taxes, 60
technology, 8, 34, 39, 41
technology gap, 41
telecommunications, 8, 52, 61, 71
telephone, 31
telephones, 31
tensions, 23, 37
tenure, 7
territorial, 41, 98
territory, 2, 4
terrorism, 37, 38, 40, 41, 44, 48, 65
terrorist acts, 41
terrorists, 38, 39, 41
textiles, 64
Thailand, 5, 23, 25, 28, 39, 46, 47, 57, 65, 67, 70, 100, 101, 104
threats, 34, 49
tin, 3, 4, 8
tobacco, 77
total energy, 103
tourism, 34
TPA, 47, 74, 92
trade, vii, viii, 3, 4, 9, 11, 12, 15, 21, 22, 24, 26, 27, 29, 30, 31, 32, 33, 34, 35, 36, 37, 41, 42, 51, 52, 54, 55, 56, 58, 60, 63, 64, 65, 66, 67, 68, 69, 71, 74, 75, 81, 92, 95, 99
trade agreement, 74
trade deficit, 27, 30, 65, 69
trade liberalization, 29, 51, 63
trade policy, 12, 29, 34, 74
Trade Policy Staff Committee, 60, 76, 91, 92
trade union, 65
trading partners, 9, 27, 71
trafficking, 22, 41, 46
training, 10, 39, 40, 41, 44
transformation, 15, 35, 36
translation, 89, 90
transmission, 101
transport, 77, 101
transportation, 6, 42
treatment, 59, 66, 93
trial, 42
Turkey, 26, 60

U

U.S. assistance, 43
U.S. Department of Commerce, 69
U.S. policy, 13
unions, 63, 65
United Kingdom, 21, 42
United Malays National Organization (UMNO), vii, 3, 6, 13, 18
United Nations (UN), 6, 9, 20, 38, 43, 48
universities, 10
Uruguay, 74
Uruguay Round, 74
USA Patriot Act, 39

V

vegetables, 78
vehicles, 26, 59, 60, 68
Vietnam, 21, 25, 26, 46, 47, 60, 64, 98
Viking, 46
violence, 16, 23
vote, vii, viii, 6, 11, 19
voters, 14
voting, 3

W

war, 4, 11, 17, 22, 37, 38, 39, 40
War on Terror, 48
Washington, 6, 37, 39, 47, 48, 49, 56, 75, 88, 90, 91
waste, 103
water, 24, 80, 97
weakness, 14
wealth, 16, 17, 29
weapons, 38
weapons of mass destruction, 38

web, 91
wells, 97, 98
Western countries, 38
White House, 36, 37, 47, 91
Wisconsin, 88
withdrawal, 19
wood, 103
workers, 22, 23, 25, 26, 52, 54, 58, 65, 66, 67, 92
working conditions, 66
working groups, 56

World Bank, 20, 24, 46, 68
World Trade Center, 46
World Trade Organization (WTO), 20, 29, 32, 34, 47, 60, 62, 63, 77, 80, 90, 92, 93
World War I, 4, 17
worldwide, 40

Y

Youth Exchange for Study (YES), 10